WORLD WAR I
IN
CARTOONS

Also by Mark Bryant

*Dictionary of British Cartoonists and Caricaturists,
1730-1980* (with S. Heneage)

*Dictionary of Twentieth-Century British Cartoonists
and Caricaturists*

Wars of Empire in Cartoons

Napoleonic Wars in Cartoons

World War II in Cartoons

God in Cartoons

The Complete Colonel Blimp (ed.)

The Comic Cruikshank (ed.)

Vicky's Supermac (ed.)

WORLD WAR I
IN
CARTOONS

Mark Bryant

GRUB STREET • LONDON

For Robert and Julius

This edition first published 2014 by
Grub Street Publishing
4 Rainham Close, London, SW11 6SS

Copyright © Mark Bryant 2006, 2014

British Library Cataloguing in Publication Data
Bryant, Mark
World War I in Cartoons
1.World War, 1914-1918 – Caricatures and cartoons
I.Title
940.3'0207

ISBN– 978-1-909808-09-6

Design by Roy Platten, Eclipse
roy.eclipse@btopenworld.com

Printed in India by Replika Press Pvt. Ltd.

CONTENTS

PREFACE

LIKE ITS COMPANION VOLUME, *World War II in Cartoons*, this book is intended primarily as a pictorial history of the Great War as seen through the eyes of the cartoonists and caricaturists who lived through it and chronicled the events as they occurred. As with the earlier book, I have added some historical background to link the images and help put them in context and, where possible, I have also supplied some information about the artists themselves and the publications (many of them now long forgotten) in which the drawings were originally published. In addition, I have once again tried to include material from both sides of the conflict but this has been limited somewhat by considerations of time and cost. Also, as before, the main emphasis has been on political and joke cartoons published in national newspapers and magazines, though material from other sources, such as books and posters, has also been included.

In the preparation of this book I am indebted to all those artists and their relatives who have helped, as well as others who have kindly supplied material, notably Pamela and Francis Wilford-Smith, Diana Willis and The World of H.M.Bateman Ltd, and Tonie and Valmai Holt. In addition I would like to thank Jenny Wood, Mike Moody and their colleagues in the Art Department of the Imperial War Museum, Nick Hiley and Jane Newton of the Centre for the Study of Cartoons & Caricature at the University of Kent, Helen Walasek and Andre Gailani of the Punch Library & Archive, Nigel Roche of the St Bride Printing Library, Peter Furtado of *History Today*, the British Library, the British Newspaper Library, the Senate House Library of the University of London, the Goethe Institute, the Institut Français, the Italian Cultural Institute, the London Press Club and all those institutions and organisations which are listed in the acknowledgements at the back of the book. Last, but by no means least, my thanks also go to John Davies, Anne Dolamore and all at Grub Street Publishing for all their support, and to the designer Roy Platten, for producing such a handsome book.

Mark Bryant
London, 2006

INTRODUCTION

FOR THOSE BROUGHT UP on computer-generated animation, graphic novels, *manga*, children's comics, Batman, Superman and the multifarious works of Disney et al., historical wartime cartoons may come as a bit of a surprise. Not only was there a wealth of material produced during World War II by artists on both sides of the conflict but a considerable amount also appeared during the Great War of 1914 to 1918.

Also, as in World War II, the impact of cartoons and caricature at this time was considerable. It should be remembered that the Great War took place not only long before the invention of the modern computer, but also before television and even radio, and the only cinema films available were black-and-white silent movies. Added to which, daily and weekly newspapers contained no colour pictures and very few carried cartoons at all. Of those that did, many no longer exist, and none of the upmarket publications in Britain – such as *The Times*, *Guardian* (then known as the *Manchester Guardian*) and the *Daily Telegraph* – published cartoons until the 1960s.

The word 'cartoon' (from the Italian *cartone*, meaning a sheet of paper or card, from which we also get the word 'carton') was originally used to describe designs or templates for tapestries, mosaics or fresco paintings, but its more widely used modern sense derives from a *Punch* spoof by John Leech of a competition for decorating the walls of the new Houses of Parliament in 1843. Classical-style cartoons sent in for the competition were exhibited in Westminster Hall and Leech attacked this as a waste of public money at a time when Londoners were starving, and headed his drawing 'Cartoon No.1'. Thereafter, the main weekly full-page topical drawing of the magazine was referred to as 'The Cartoon' and the word gradually came to be applied to comic or satirical drawings generally.

The art form itself, of course – together with that of caricature (from another Italian word, *caricare*, meaning to overburden or exaggerate) – has a long history going back to Ancient Egypt, but it became increasingly popular from the 18th century onwards with the works of Hogarth, Gillray, Rowlandson and Cruikshank in Britain and such overseas masters as Daumier, Wilhelm Busch, and others.

However, though cartoonists had chronicled the Napoleonic Wars in individually produced prints (often hand-coloured) it was with the arrival of specialist journals containing cartoons in the 19th century that their impact really began to be felt by all sections of society. *La Caricature* (1830) and *Le Charivari* (1832) in France, *Punch* (1841) and *Vanity Fair* (1868) in England, *Kladderadatsch* (1848) and *Simplicissimus* (1896) in Germany, and *Puck* (1876) and *Judge* (1881) in the USA – among many others – all published cartoons regularly. And in 1890, after two years as a freelance contributor, Francis Carruthers Gould joined the London evening newspaper, the *Pall Mall Gazette* (which then had a similar readership to the *Evening Standard* today) as the first ever staff cartoonist working for a daily newspaper.

This was the period of John Tenniel, Thomas Nast, George du Maurier, Max Beerbohm, 'Ape', 'Spy', 'Caran D'Ache', Linley Sambourne, Phil May and others. The topics they covered for most of the 19th century were small colonial wars and society figures, but from the Franco-Prussian War of 1870-71 and with the rise of Prussian military might, this began to change.

By the time of the outbreak of the Great War in August 1914, a number of regional and national daily and weekly newspapers regularly published topical and political cartoons. In Britain these included such familiar names as the *Daily Express*, the *Daily Mirror* (the biggest selling daily paper in the UK by 1914) and the *Daily Mail*, which became the official paper of the troops, 10,000 copies being sent to the front line every day. Other popular newspapers of the time included some now long-forgotten, such as the *Daily Graphic*, *Daily Sketch*, *Daily Herald* and *Daily Chronicle*, evening papers such as the *Evening News*, *Star* and *Westminster Gazette*, and weeklies such as the *Weekly Dispatch*, *Reynolds News* and *Sunday Graphic*. In addition, in Britain there were magazines such as *Punch*, the *Bystander*, *Tatler*, *Humorist*, *London Opinion*, *Sketch* and *John Bull* with their overseas equivalents such as the *Sydney Bulletin* and *Melbourne Punch* (Australia), *De Nieuwe Amsterdammer* (Holland), *Le Rire* (France), *Mucha* (Poland), *Il 420* (Italy), *Hindi Punch* (India), *Die Muskete* (Austria) and *Jugend* and *Ulk* (Germany). During the war itself new magazines were founded including *Le Canard Enchaîné* (1915) in France and *The Passing Show* (1915) and *Blighty* (1916) in Britain and in 1918 the US Government even set up a Bureau of Cartoons which published a weekly specialist journal, *Bulletin for Cartoonists* (1918).

With these publications came a number of already established cartoonists. In Britain these included Sidney Strube on the *Daily Express*, Jack Walker on the *Daily Graphic*, the Australian Will Dyson on the *Daily Herald*, W.K.Haselden on the *Daily Mirror*, W.H.Toy on the *Daily Sketch*, Poy (Percy Fearon) on the *Daily Mail* and *Evening News*, G.A.Stevens on the *Star* and such magazine artists as Bert Thomas (*London Opinion*), and regular *Punch* contributors like Bernard Partridge, F.H.Townsend, Frank Reynolds, Leonard Raven Hill, E.H.Shepard and H.M.Bateman.

The war itself produced plenty of opportunities for jokes – after all, the Battle of Mons in 1915 was the first battle the British Army had fought in Europe since Waterloo and there had been many advances in technology since then. New inventions such as submarines, aeroplanes, gasmasks, Zeppelins and tanks all lent themselves to cartoons as did trench warfare and goose-stepping Germans with their *pickelhaube* helmets and *wurst* etc. However, a number of jokes would not seem so funny today. Not only did many still have long-winded captions in the Victorian style but the topics themselves would be less acceptable in these politically correct times – especially sexist and racist gags and those relating to class consciousness. Added to which the Great War gave rise to a large number of so-called 'hate' cartoons featuring gruesome pictures of babies being bayoneted and other kinds of real or imagined atrocity. These cartoons are far from funny and were produced by artists on both sides of the conflict.

Caricature also featured widely in the Great War. The early years of the century had seen the slow transformation of cartoon conventions with national symbols such as Britannia, Marianne, Uncle Sam and John Bull – as well as the British Lion, the Russian Bear, the French Cockerel etc – gradually giving way to portraits of heads of state. By the outbreak of the Great War the national leaders were a gift to cartoonists. On the side of the Central Powers were Kaiser Wilhelm with his flamboyant uniforms and upturned moustache, the bull-necked General Hindenburg, Admiral von Tirpitz with his strange twin-pointed beard, the doddering Emperor Franz Joseph of Austria-Hungary with his huge mutton-chop whiskers and the large-nosed King Ferdinand of Bulgaria. And amongst the Allies were Lord Kitchener with his stiff military bearing; the tall, thin and bespectacled President Wilson of the USA; Clemenceau and Poincaré of France with their distinctive beards; and the moustache and twinkling eyes of Britain's Prime Minister Lloyd George.

Many pre-war cartoonists served their country and saw action in the Great War and some achieved high rank or were decorated for valour. For example *Punch*'s main sporting cartoonist, G.D.Armour, became a lieutenant-colonel and was awarded an OBE, two others received MBEs, two received the Military Cross and another Punch artist, Arthur Watts, took part in the Zeebrugge Raid and was twice awarded the DSO. Some also added to their duties by working as official war artists. Amongst these was Will Dyson who was attached to the Australian forces and William Heath Robinson who drew the American Expeditionary Force in France in the spring of 1918.

A number of British cartoonists also made their reputations during this period and created memorable characters. These included Bruce Bairnsfather, whose walrus-moustached veteran Tommy 'Old Bill' became one of the most famous British images of the period, along with Haselden's 'Big and Little Willie' series (which the Kaiser himself reputedly said had been 'damnably effective'), Alfred Leete's 'Schmidt the Spy' and Kitchener poster, and the celebrated cartoon ''Arf a Mo', Kaiser' by Bert Thomas who was awarded an MBE for his war work. E.H.Shepard (later of *Winnie the Pooh* fame), won a Military Cross at Ypres in the war and achieved the rank of major, and Kenneth Bird, the only cartoonist ever to become Editor of *Punch*, also came to prominence at this time. He began drawing for *Punch* in 1916 after being shot in the spine at Gallipoli and his pseudonym 'Fougasse' came from the French word for a small anti-personnel mine ('Its effectiveness is not always reliable and its aim uncertain').

Cartoonists on both sides of the conflict also produced posters and a number of animated cartoon films were made for propaganda purposes, including (in Britain) *The U-Tube* by Lancelot Speed and Tom Webster's *Charlie at The Front* (1918) and (in the USA) Winsor McCay's *The Sinking of the Lusitania* (1918). However, this graphic scrapbook of the Great War concentrates on newspaper and magazine cartoons for the simple reason that these would have been the most widely seen by the public at the time. The only difficulty here, though, is that by their very nature daily newspaper cartoons are ephemeral and the publications they appeared in were usually thrown away by the following day. Hence the present compendium which, it is hoped, will preserve some of them for posterity.

PRE-WAR

WITH MANY WARS throughout history, the seeds of dissent that cause the final outbreak of hostilities are often sown in the ruins and humiliations of previous conflicts. The Great War of 1914-18 (only known in hindsight as World War I) was no exception. Amongst the many contributing factors was the rise of an aggressive military policy in Germany and the belief that its allegedly superior *Kultur* (culture) should be imposed on other supposedly benighted countries – a belief which had been fuelled by Prussia's success in the Franco-Prussian War of 1870-71.

For most of the 19th century the world had been ruled by huge empires – Russia, France, Austria-Hungary, Great Britain and Turkey (the Ottoman Empire) – and the balance of power had been assured by a number of mutual defensive treaties. However, in 1870, Napoleon III of France unwisely declared war on Prussia – a country which had become increasingly strong under its new king, Wilhelm I, and his dynamic Prime Minister, Otto von Bismarck. Under their leadership Prussia had become the dominant force in Germany and had had impressive military successes against Denmark (1864) and Austria (1866). Thus, when the French were finally beaten in the Franco-Prussian War at the Battle of Sedan, Wilhelm declared himself *Kaiser* (caesar, tsar or emperor) of the whole of the new German Empire with Bismarck as his Chancellor.

On Wilhelm's death in 1888 he was succeeded by his grandson, Kaiser Wilhelm II, who continued Germany's expansionist military policies and, after sacking Bismarck in 1890, took an increasing personal interest in affairs of state. Britain also had considerable influence in Europe at this time as Queen Victoria (herself of German origins) was the grandmother of the new Kaiser and great-aunt of Tsar Nicholas II of Russia, and thus on his succession in 1901 her son Edward VII became known as the 'Uncle of All Europe'. Added to which, most royal families in Europe were interlinked by marriage. This should have made for extreme stability. However, ethnic tensions within the Austro-Hungarian Empire (which also contained Czechs, Slovaks, Poles, Slovenes, Croats and Serbs) and the Ottoman Empire (including Armenians and Arabs) – as well as massive rearmament by Germany – led to international unrest.

In addition, tensions in other parts of the world also had an effect on Europe (and vice-versa) as the rapid rise in colonialism over the previous century meant that by 1914 more than 80 per cent of the globe was controlled by European powers. Amongst these factors were Britain's involvement in the Boer War (1899-1902) – which was opposed by both France and Germany (each of whom had colonies in Africa) and diplomatic incidents involving France, Italy and Germany in Morocco and Libya. Added to which were the growing power of Japan – which, freed from 250 years of isolationism, had had considerable success in the Russo-Japanese War (1904-05) – and victories by the Balkan League (Bulgaria, Serbia and Greece) against the Ottoman Empire (1912-13).

It would only take a spark to ignite the biggest conflagration the world had ever seen. That spark proved to be the assassination of the Archduke Franz Ferdinand, heir to the throne of Austria-Hungary, by Serbian nationalists in Sarajevo, capital of what was then the Austro-Hungarian province of Bosnia.

The Franco-Prussian War (1870-71) ended in disaster for the French. At the Battle of Sedan in September 1870 the entire French Army of 124,000 men surrendered. This was the worst French defeat ever until World War II. Soon afterwards Napoleon III abdicated and King Wilhelm I of Prussia was crowned Kaiser of the new German Empire in the Hall of Mirrors at the Palace of Versailles near Paris, former residence of France's most famous ruler, the 'Sun King' Louis XIV. This insult and the loss of the provinces of Alsace and Lorraine to Germany by the Treaty of Frankfurt in 1871 would long linger in French memories and would resurface during the Great War.

After the Franco-Prussian War Bismarck was made a prince and Chancellor (Prime Minister) of the new German Empire. He was known as the 'Iron Chancellor', after his first speech as Chancellor to the Reichstag (Parliament) in 1862 in which he said: 'The great questions of our day cannot be solved by speeches and majority votes [...] but by blood and iron.' In 1879, to counteract the Entente between Russia and France he signed the Treaty of Alliance between Germany and the Austro-Hungarian Empire, which Italy joined in 1886 to form the Triple Alliance.

The drawing reproduced here *(right)* is by James Tissot (1836-1902), who drew a number of caricatures for *Vanity Fair* under the pseudonym 'Coïdé' from 1869 to 1877.

The Ablest Statesman in Europe
Coïdé (James Tissot), *Vanity Fair*, 15 October 1870

Au Revoir
Germany: 'Farewell, Madam, and if...'
France: 'Ha! We shall meet again!'
John Tenniel, *Punch*, 27 September 1873

The cartoon by Tenniel *(left)* hints prophetically at the conflict still to come and was reproduced in *Punch* at the end of the Great War, on 20 November 1918. John Tenniel (1820-1914), who became the main artist on *Punch* in 1864 and was knighted in 1893, was perhaps best known as the illustrator of Lewis Carroll's *Alice's Adventures in Wonderland* (1865) and other books. He died on 25 February 1914, the year the Great War broke out.

DROPPING THE PILOT.

Dropping the Pilot
John Tenniel, *Punch*, 29 March 1890

With the death of Wilhelm I in 1888 and the accession of his grandson Wilhelm II (whose mother was Queen Victoria's daughter, Victoria) Bismarck's power began to wane until he was dismissed by the Kaiser in 1890. Tenniel's cartoon from *Punch* has Wilhelm watching Bismarck as a ship's pilot who is shown symbolically leaving the ship of state now that his job is done. Reproduced over two pages of the magazine, it is one of *Punch*'s most famous images and has been the subject of numerous pastiches over the years.

In retirement Bismarck spent many years writing his memoirs, parts of which were suppressed for a time because of their criticism of Wilhelm II. The French caricature *(below)* by Moloch (Alphonse Hector Colomb, 1848-1909) has been drawn in the style of a silhouette. (Note the three hairs on Bismarck's head which became a symbol for him.)

Bismarck Prepares to Write His Memoirs
Moloch (Alphonse Hector Colomb), c.1890

With Bismarck no longer in control, Wilhelm II soon began to take over direct rule and was keen to expand the German Empire still further. In the first cartoon *(right)* by Linley Sambourne the reference is to the character Fidgety Philip from *Struwwelpeter* (1845), the popular nineteenth-century German collection of moral tales by Heinrich Hoffmann. In this case Wilhelm is seen as the child who is upsetting his associates of the Triple Alliance – Italy (centre) and Austria-Hungary's Emperor Franz Joseph.

In the second drawing *(below)* Wilhelm is seen imagining himself in a 'new role' as Emperor of China, having just negotiated a treaty to lease Kiaochow (and its port Tsingtao) in the Chinese province of Shantung for 99 years. Tsingtao (now Qingdao) soon became Germany's main military base in the Far East. (*Le Voyage en Chine* [1865] was a comic opera by François Bazin.)

Linley Sambourne (1845-1910), who succeeded Tenniel as chief cartoonist of *Punch* in 1901, was a relative of Princess Margaret's first husband – Anthony Armstrong-Jones, Viscount Linley and Earl of Snowdon. Both these cartoons were later reprinted on 16 September 1914 in a special wartime *Punch* supplement on the Kaiser entitled 'The New Rake's Progress'.

The Story of Fidgety Wilhelm
Linley Sambourne, *Punch*, 1 February 1896

A New Role
Imperial 'Manager -Actor' (who has cast himself for a leading part in *Un Voyage en Chine*, *sotto voce*):
'Um-ha! With just a few additional touches here and there, I shall make a first-rate Emperor of China!'
Linley Sambourne, *Punch*, 15 January 1898

N° 265. 6ᵉ année. 2 Décembre 1899.   15 centimes.

Le Rire

JOURNAL HUMORISTIQUE PARAISSANT LE SAMEDI

Un an : Paris, 8 fr.
Départements. 9 fr. Étranger, 11 fr.
Six mois : France, 5 fr. Étranger, 6 fr.

M. Félix JUVEN, Directeur. — Partie artistique : M. Arsène ALEXANDRE

La reproduction des dessins du RIRE est absolument interdite aux publications, françaises ou étrangères, sans autorisation

10, rue Saint-Joseph, 10
PARIS

Les manuscrits et dessins non insérés ne sont pas rendus.

Guillaume II recevant, au Lustgarden, le serment des nouvelles recrues, leur a dit d'une voix retentissante : « Un homme n'a qu'une parole ! » La parole de l'empereur d'Allemagne a été engagée en 1896.   (*Les Journaux*.)

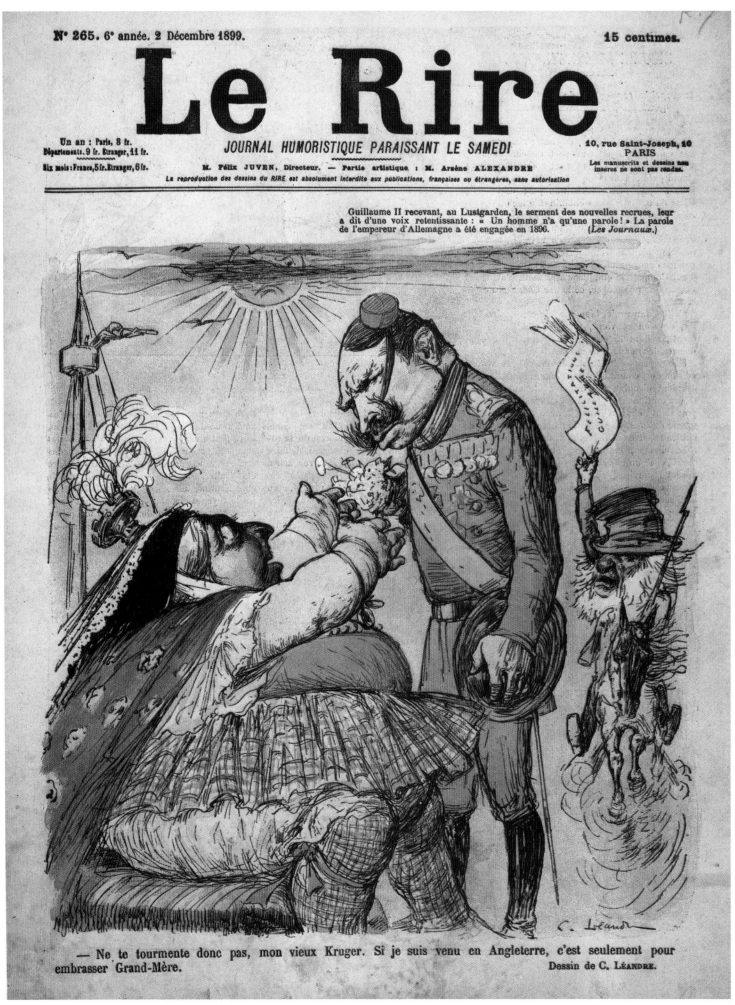

— Ne te tourmente donc pas, mon vieux Kruger. Si je suis venu en Angleterre, c'est seulement pour embrasser Grand-Mère.

Dessin de C. LÉANDRE.

'Don't be concerned, my dear Kruger. I am only going to England to visit my grandmother.'
Charles Léandre, *Le Rire* (Paris), 2 December 1899

In 1899 the Kaiser supported the Dutch Boer uprising in South Africa against the British as Germany had aspirations for building an empire in Africa. The French were also anti-British during the Boer War and in the colour cartoon by Charles Léandre (1862-1930) from the front cover of *Le Rire* magazine *(left)*, the Kaiser (dressed as a British Tommy) is shown during his visit to Britain in November 1899. To prevent any mistake about his loyalties in Africa he says he is visiting his grandmother, Queen Victoria. Meanwhile, at the right of the picture, Paul Kruger (President of the Transvaal and leader of the Boers), desperately tries to prevent him doing so. In his hand Kruger waves the infamous Kruger Telegram the Kaiser had sent in 1896, which soured Anglo-German relations. (The telegram had congratulated Kruger on defeating an attempted coup in the Transvaal by British forces – the so-called Jameson Raid.)

In another powerful anti-British cartoon *(right)*, the French artist Jean Veber (1864-1928) depicts the overweight newly crowned king Edward VII as a barrel crushing innocent victims. It was published in a special edition of *L'Assiette au Beurre* devoted to the concentration camps that the British had created in South Africa during the Boer War. The king's corpulence – as well as his amorous adventures – are also commented on in the second cartoon from *L'Assiette au Beurre* showing British troops marching at his funeral *(below right)*.

Meanwhile, Sambourne's British view of the conflict *(below left)* has Germany arming Kruger. This cartoon carried a quotation from the popular London evening newspaper the *Globe* from 13 April 1897, which read: 'The *Vossische Zeitung* chronicles with satisfaction the recent arrival at Lorenzo Marques, on board the German East African liner *Kaiser*, of 1,650 cases of war material for the Transvaal, including a whole battery of heavy guns, and states its conviction that the Transvaal and the Orange Free State are "determined to maintain their independence".' This cartoon was later reproduced in a special supplement to *Punch* called '*Punch* and the Prussian Bully' published on 14 October 1914.

The Thunderbolt of War
Jean Veber, *L'Assiette au Beurre* (Paris), 28 September 1901

True Popularity
'When we were sent off to the colonies, they told us:
"You must use all means possible to make the British Empire
bigger, stronger and more populated!"'
'That's right, Tommy, and the great King Edward
himself led by example!'
L'Assiette au Beurre (Paris), 4 June 1910

Germania Arming Kruger
Linley Sambourne, *Punch*, 24 April 1897

It would be a mistake to think that the international image of Germany has always been one of a belligerent nation of goose-stepping soldiers wearing *pickelhaube* helmets. More commonly, especially in Bavaria and the south of Germany, they had been traditionally seen in the terms of Spitzweg's kindly philosopher *(left)* with his Tyrolean-style pipe. And the relaxed lager-drinking soldier from *Fliegende Blätter (below)* is in marked contrast to the troops of Bismarck's day. Note the storks nesting in his hat (which has also been transformed into a beehive) and the ivy creeping up his musket, a sign of complete inactivity.

Carl Spitzweg, c.1850

Armed Peace
Fliegende Blätter, c.1850

The Giant Michel and the Dwarf Wilhelm
'The dwarf thinks himself big because he can spit a long way' – *Old Proverb*
Edmund J.Sullivan, *The Kaiser's Garland* (1915)

French postcard,1914

First Lessons in the Goose Step
William Heath Robinson, *Some 'Frightful' War Pictures* (1915)

These three drawings make fun of the transition to militarism under Kaiser Wilhelm. In the cartoon by Sullivan *(above)* a tiny Wilhelm sits astride the neck of a modern, bloated, version of Germany's national figure Michael (or Michel) – the equivalent of England's John Bull – who continues to drink his beer and blow smoke rings from his Bavarian pipe.

Edmund Sullivan (1869-1933) later went on to become President of the Art Workers' Guild, a distinguished book illustrator and a teacher of illustration and lithography at Goldsmiths' School of Art, whose pupils included Sir Graham Sutherland and Eric Fraser. This drawing is from his powerful wartime collection *The Kaiser's Garland* (1915).

In the cartoon by William Heath Robinson (1872-1944) *(right)*, famous for his drawings of crazy machines, a gosling teaches a group of overweight new German recruits how to march in goose-step.

Meanwhile, the French postcard *(above right)* shows an elderly member of the Bavarian infantry.

F.H.Townsend, *Punch's Almanack for 1915*, December 1914

The Kaiser's Dream: The End of the World
Jack Walker, *The Daily Graphic Special War Cartoons, No.2* (1914)

Amongst the many factors involved with the rise of 'kaiserism' (as it became known) was its support by German intellectuals. The imposition of what was felt to be the superior German culture (*Kultur*) onto other countries was seen as a benevolent act. Even as late as 22 October 1914, the President of the Prussian Diet declared that the German armies were engaged in the fulfilment of 'the great *Kultur*-mission of the German people among the nations of the earth'. This was supported by patriotic historians such as the Berlin professor and Reichstag member Heinrich von Treischke and the retired general Friedrich von Bernhardi (1849-1930), one of Germany's most notable military theorists. Bernhardi came to prominence in 1912 after publishing a book called *Germany and the Next War* (translated into English and widely read in Britain) in which he said that a European war was inevitable, that Germany must either conquer or die and that she should thus build armaments and train soldiers as quickly as possible and to the utmost of her ability. It caused a sensation in Britain and did much to promote the idea of Germany's aggressive intentions.

The drawing by Townsend *(left)* shows Bernhardi, armed to the teeth (literally) as he writes his book between busts of Bismarck (left) and the Kaiser (right). Behind him are maps of Armageddon (the name given in the Bible's Book of Revelations to the site of the last 'great battle of that great day of God almighty' between the forces of good and evil) and Golders Green (a largely Jewish area of London) as the site for concrete bases for field guns.

The cartoon *(below left)* by Jack Walker (fl.1914-21) in the *Daily Graphic* (Britain's first ever pictorial daily morning newspaper) shows the Kaiser about to eat Britain, having already consumed almost half the globe. On the table is a bottle of 'Bernhardi's Sauce' whose label reads: 'Produces a Prodigious Appetite'.

Sullivan's drawing *(right)* has Bernhardi's book upon which sits the Kaiser's skull topped by the skeleton of the German imperial eagle between which hangs a spider's web to denote the lack of activity. The torn-up paper and royal seal indicate the destruction of Germany's treaty guaranteeing Belgium's neutrality.

Meanwhile, Francis Carruthers Gould (1844-1925) lampoons the Kaiser's many moods *(below)*. Gould was the first ever staff political cartoonist on a daily newspaper and began at the *Pall Mall Gazette* before moving to the newly launched *Westminster Gazette* in 1893. During the Great War he also produced a series of Toby Jug pottery caricatures of prominent wartime figures including Lloyd George, Woodrow Wilson, Haig, French and Joffre. He was knighted in 1906.

Edmund J.Sullivan, *The Kaiser's Garland* (1915)

Phases and Faces
Different views of the Kaiser suggested by various newspapers during the last week or two
F.C.Gould, *Westminster Gazette*, 14 October 1905

19

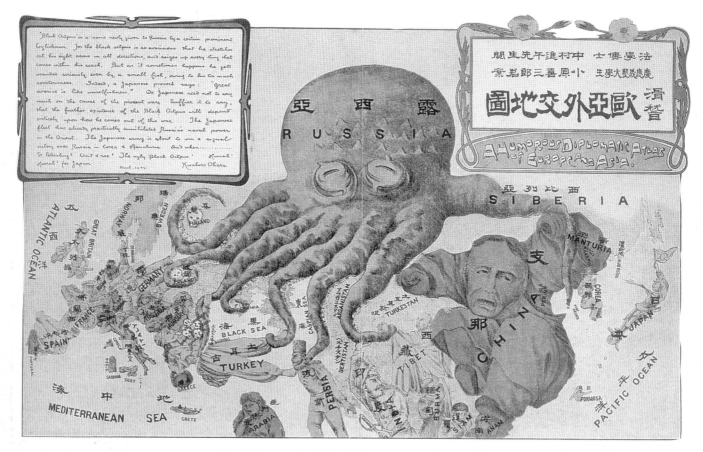

A Humorous Map of Europe and Asia
Kisaburo Ohara, 1906

By the end of the first decade of the 20th century, international relations had become very unstable. As well as Germany, another country which had become a significant player on the world stage was Japan. In 1868, after 250 years of isolation under the dictatorial rule of the military *shoguns*, the imperial throne was restored and Japan's borders were opened. The Russo-Japanese War (1904-1905) was the first major international conflict of the 20th century and, to the surprise of many, the Russians were soundly beaten at the Battle of Tsushima. It was a staggering lesson to Russia, one of the world's greatest empires.

The cartoon map *(above)* shows a Japanese view of Russian dominance. (Note that the Russian octopus already has its tentacles around China, Tibet, Persia, Turkey, Poland and Finland.)

Meanwhile, in central and southern Europe things were also reaching boiling point. Turkey at this time was known as the 'Sick Man of Europe' and in 1908, after Bulgaria had broken away from the fast-crumbling Ottoman Empire and Austria-Hungary had annexed the former Turkish regions of Bosnia and Herzegovina, a group known as the Young Turks seized power in an attempt to transform the country into a modern European state. They deposed Sultan Abdul Hamid and replaced him in 1909 with his brother Mohammed (Mehmet) V but Turkey's troubles continued. In the Italo-Turkish War (1911-12), Turkey lost a large part of Ottoman-controlled Libya to Italy and soon afterwards Bulgaria, Serbia and Greece formed the Balkan League and attacked Turkey during the Balkan Wars (1912-1913), resulting in the loss of still more Turkish territory. Reforms then began to be made and German military advisers started to train the Turkish Army, leading to secret negotiations with Germany after Enver Pasha (former Turkish military attaché to Berlin) became Minister of War in 1913 (though when the Great War broke out Turkey was still officially neutral).

The two cartoons by F.H.Townsend refer to the Germanisation of Turkey and the imminent threat of world war sparked off from the powder-keg of the Balkans region. F.H.Townsend (1868-1920) was the first ever Art Editor of *Punch* (1905). He was the brother-in-law of a fellow *Punch* cartoonist, Frank Reynolds, and served in the Special Constabulary during the Great War. The first drawing *(below)* shows a goose-stepping Turkey with a *pickelhaube* helmet as the Kaiser looks on, while the second one *(opposite)* shows the bleak outlook for world peace as 1913 dawns.

The Teutonising of Turkey
German Kaiser: 'Good Bird!'
F.H.Townsend, *Punch*, 5 October 1910

Sheltering the New Year
F.H.Townsend, *Punch*, December 1912

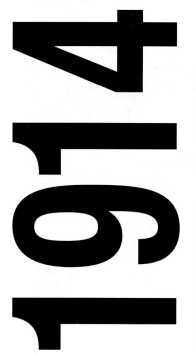

1914

ON SUNDAY 28 JUNE 1914, the 14th anniversary of his wedding (and by coincidence the National Day of Serbia), Archduke Franz Ferdinand, heir to the throne of the Austro-Hungarian Empire and Inspector-General of the Imperial Army, took his wife Sophie with him on an official tour of Sarajevo, capital of the Austro-Hungarian province of Bosnia-Herzegovina. While travelling in an open carriage he and his wife were killed by three shots fired by Gabril Princip, a member of the Black Hand gang of Bosnian Serb nationalists. Believing that Serbia itself was closely involved with the outrage, Austria immediately demanded justice and sent an ultimatum to Belgrade. However, ignoring Serbia's abject apologies, Austria-Hungary declared war on 28 July and thereby began a process that made the Great War inevitable.

The immediate consequence was a series of military mobilisations by other countries linked to both sides by mutual treaties of support, which resulted in the alignment of the Central Powers (Germany and Austria-Hungary) against the Triple Entente Allies of Russia, France and Great Britain. Then when neutral Belgium refused to allow German troops to cross into France, the Kaiser reneged on treaties Germany had signed guaranteeing Belgian neutrality and invaded the country. Subsequently, in the first week of August 1914, Britain and France honoured their pacts with Belgium and declared war on Germany, and when the following week Austro-Hungarian troops invaded Serbia, the Allies declared war on Austria-Hungary as well. By the end of August Japan had also joined in on the side of the Allies and in October Turkey joined the Central Powers.

At first the Belgians put up a spirited resistance to the massive German assault of half a million troops but were soon overwhelmed as the Kaiser's generals reached the French border and began to implement their pre-war strategy known as the Schlieffen Plan, aimed at knocking out France in six weeks before turning to attack Russia. Meanwhile, the French had begun to carry out their own pre-war plan to attack Germany via Alsace-Lorraine and the so-called 'Battle of the Frontiers' commenced. However, after the Battle of the Marne outside Paris, the rapid advances of the German Army were suddenly halted and replaced by trench warfare. On the Eastern Front, though the Russians had considerable initial success against the Austro-Hungarian Army in Galicia (part of modern Poland), their invasion of East Prussia in northern Germany resulted in a disastrous defeat for them at the Battle of Tannenberg.

Things were not going much better for the Allies at sea. Though the Royal Navy had had some success at the Battle of Heligoland Bight (off the coast of Denmark), it lost two cruisers at the Battle of Coronel in the Pacific, and was being harassed by the new menaces of German mines and submarines (U-boats). Civilians at home in England were also targeted for the first time, with long-range bombing attacks by Zeppelin airships and the shelling of coastal towns by heavy cruisers of the Imperial German Navy.

However, the year ended on a bright note for the Allies – as well as capturing German colonies in Africa and the Pacific they began to advance into Turkish-ruled Mesopotamia (modern Iraq) and the Caucasus. There was also an unofficial Christmas Truce on the Western Front during which troops on the opposing sides fraternised and even played football together.

European Cuisine
Russian print, c.1914

The USA tried to broker a peace agreement to avoid world war and the anonymous Russian cartoon 'European Cuisine' *(left)* shows the various countries that took part in the conflict as culinary national stereotypes while above all flies the peacemaking American eagle. Left to right, these include the many peoples of the Russian stewpot attacking the two small sausages chained together representing Austria-Hungary, a Turkey leg (with warships as shoes), Germany (the large sausage getting burnt as it tries to cook the roast beef of England) and France (the bottle of champagne). Note the box marked 'Kiao-Chau' (Kiaochow, the important German Far East base leased from China).

Sir Edward Grey
Tom Titt (Jan Stanislaw de Junosza
Rosciszewski), *Caricatures* (1913)

Infelix Austria! – What Next?
Arthur Johnson, *Kladderadatsch* (Berlin), 1914

On 29 July 1914, in the first military action of the Great War, Austro-Hungarian warships on the Danube bombarded Belgrade, the Serbian capital. However, three separate invasions of the country in August, September and November were repulsed by the Serbs. Many also doubted the wisdom of Austria-Hungary's declaration of war, knowing that Russia was bound to come to the aid of a fellow Slav nation. However, Austria knew that it could also count on the support of Kaiser Wilhelm's militaristic Germany which was becoming increasingly powerful in Europe. The motto of the Habsburg Dynasty was 'Felix Austria' (Happy Austria) but many of the family had died violently over the past 50 years. The German cartoon depicting the figure of Death *(above right)* was published in Berlin soon after the assassination of Franz Ferdinand.

On hearing that peace negotiations had failed British Foreign Secretary Sir Edward Grey, watching a lamplighter at work in London's St James's Park from the window of his room in the Foreign Office, said: 'The lamps are going out all over Europe; we shall not see them lit again in our lifetime.' (However, there was a certain irony as Grey left office in 1916 because of his failing eyesight.)

The drawing of Grey *(above left)* by the Polish-born caricaturist 'Tom Titt' (Jan Stanislaw de Junosza Rosciszewski, 1885-1965) originally appeared in the weekly *New Age*, which published a collection of his work in 1913.

Austria: '**That settles it! Now I shall be under the painful necessity of punishing you.**'
Jack Walker, *The Daily Graphic Special War Cartoons, No.1* (1914)

'S is a scrap – made of paper, of course'
G.A.Stevens in S.Lupton and G.A.Stevens,
An English ABC for Little Willie and Others (c.1915)

The Self-Starter Worked All Right
Luther Bradley, *Chicago Daily News*, 15 September 1914

Having occupied Luxembourg two days earlier, the Germany Imperial Army commanded by Field Marshal Helmut von Moltke (nephew of the hero of the Franco-Prussian War) marched into Belgium on 4 August 1914. In so doing Germany reneged on two treaties (1839 and 1871) which it had signed (with Britain) to guarantee the country's neutrality. Believing that Britain would stay neutral despite this the German Chancellor, Theobald von Bethmann-Hollweg, could not believe it when Prime Minister Herbert Asquith declared war on Germany the same day. As Bethmann-Hollweg said to Sir Edward Goschen, the British ambassador in Berlin: 'Just for a word, "neutrality" – a word that in wartime has so often been disregarded – just for the sake of a scrap of paper Great Britain is going to make war on a kindred nation, which desires nothing better than to be friends with her.'

The illustration by G.A.Stevens political cartoonist of the *Star*, *(above left)*, shows the Kaiser's disdain for such treaties while 'War' *(below right)* was published in the Italian Socialist daily *Avanti!* (then edited by the future dictator, Benito Mussolini) before neutral Italy joined the Allies. Jean Veber's drawing *(below left)* shows the French view of the giant German military machine as it storms across Europe. Luther Bradley (1853-1917) was against the USA's entry into the Great War and died on 9 January 1917, four months before this happened. In his drawing *(above right)* note the sign on the tree saying 'Bankruptcy This Way.'

The Beast is Unleashed
Jean Veber, August 1914

War
Giuseppe Scalarini, *Avanti!* (Rome), 7 August 1914

Bravo, Belgium!
F.H.Townsend, *Punch*, 12 August 1914

Though at first overwhelmed by the German onslaught the Belgians quickly rallied and even with their comparatively tiny forces managed to fight back. The image of this David and Goliath battle is shown in the *Punch* cartoon by F.H.Townsend *(above)*, one of the most famous cartoons of the Great War. It shows Germany personified as the kindly old man of pre-war German stereotypes (note the sausages in his pocket and the Bavarian pipe) but armed this time with a stick. Belgium, meanwhile, is depicted as a little farm boy wearing smock and clogs and brandishing a smaller stick in the hope of barring his way to the field and the village (with its church) beyond.

The Heroic Deed of Kozma Kryuchkov the Bogatyr
Russian print, c.1914

Meanwhile, on the Eastern Front, Russian forces advanced into German territory in East Prussia in the north on 17 August and the Austro-Hungarian province of Galicia (now Poland) in the south. At first the Russians had great success but once the German commander in the area was replaced by General Paul von Hindenburg, who was called up out of retirement, the tables were turned completely. By 31 August the Germans had stopped the Russians in their tracks at Tannenberg (modern Stebark, Poland, 100 miles north of Warsaw) and had taken 120,000 prisoners in a major victory. Hindenburg and his chief-of-staff, Erich von Ludendorff, also later inflicted further heavy defeats on the Russians in East Prussia at the Battle of the Masurian Lakes.

The cartoon by Jack Walker *(below)* shows the British view of the initial success of the 'Russian steamroller' as it drives the German dachshund westwards, while the Russian print *(above)* shows Cossacks impaling German troops. The elite Cossack cavalry had a fearsome reputation and this print records the deeds of one hero who, with three colleagues, attacked 27 German cavalrymen. Kozma bayoneted 11 of them and was himself wounded 16 times. For this he received the Cross of St George.

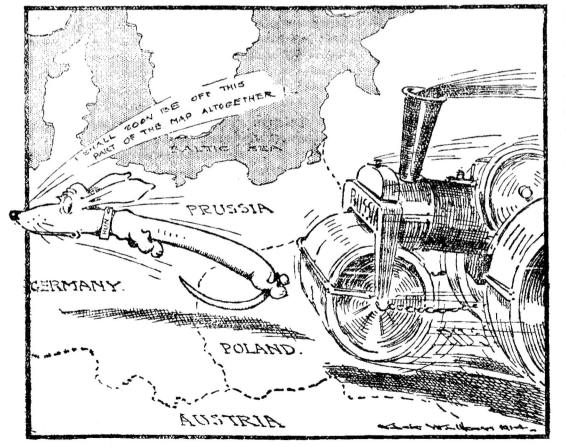

The Steam Roller Gets Going
Jack Walker, *The Daily Graphic Special War Cartoons, No.4* (1914)

However, the later situation is summed up by the German comic map of Europe *(below)*, which shows Germany's national figure Michael punching Russia with his left hand while his right (a mailed fist seen coming out of the North Sea) attacks Britain. (Note the inset detail of Japan in the Pacific Ocean.)

The Russian poster *(right)*, meanwhile, depicts Kaiser Wilhelm as a crazed cavalryman riding a wild boar and accompanied by vampire bats and mad dachshund dogs wearing *pickelhaube* helmets (the Kaiser owned a number of dachshunds) as he lays waste to the countryside with such fury that his imperial crown has fallen off. Note also that this is one of very few cartoons which alludes to the Kaiser's withered left arm. This can be seen as a collection of mere bones which hold a field marshal's baton. The arm is itself being held by the tail of a goblin which is holding the harness of the boar to prevent the Kaiser falling off.

The German Anti-Christ
Russian Poster, c.1914

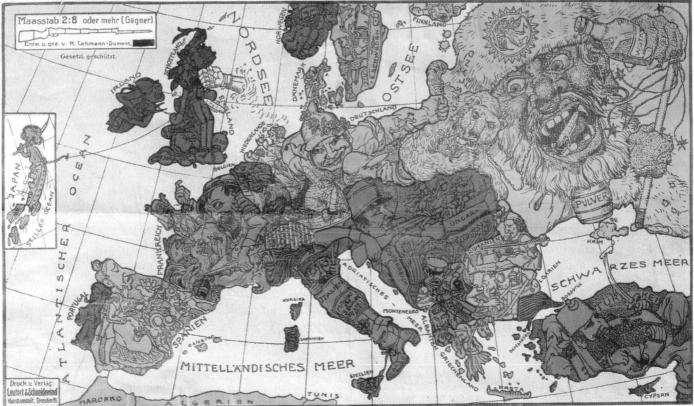

A Humorous Map of Europe in the Year 1914
German print by Leutert & Schneidewind (Dresden), c.1914

The Belgians put up a spirited resistance to the German attack but, faced with the biggest invasion force ever seen in history, were no match for the Kaiser's troops. Their first target was the fortified city of Liège (Belgium's biggest industrial centre) which blocked the crossing of the Meuse and defended the route to Brussels. At first this proved a tough nut to crack and the Germans suffered heavy casualties. But when they brought up immense siege guns the 12 great forts surrounding Liège soon fell, followed by those in Namur. The biggest German gun – nicknamed 'Dicke Berta' ('Big Bertha'), after the rotund wife of Gustav von Bohlen, head of the Krupp steelworks – could fire 42cm (16½ inch) shells.

Louis Raemaekers *(left)* draws Big Bertha talking to Britannia as she plans another assault (Flushing is modern Vlissingen in Holland). Though a Dutchman, Raemaekers' gruesome cartoons were widely published in British and French newspapers and led to his prosecution by the Dutch authorities for endangering their neutrality. As a result he came to England in 1915 where Prime Minister Lloyd George was so impressed by his drawings that he persuaded him to go to the USA in an effort to enlist American help in the war. The famous *Times* correspondent Sir Harry Perry Robinson held that he was one of six great men – including statesmen and military commanders – whose effort and influence were most decisive during the Great War.

Jack Walker's cartoon *(below left)* was drawn at a time when the Belgians seemed to be holding off the Germans.

On Concrete Foundations
Big Bertha: 'What a charming view over Flushing Harbour!
May I build a villa here?'
Louis Raemaekers, c.1915

The Cure
Dame Europa: 'There's nothing like a poultice or two
for a swelled head, William.'
Jack Walker, *The Daily Graphic Special War Cartoons, No 1* (1914)

After Liège and Namur the Germans headed for Brussels and King Albert moved his court and the Government to Antwerp. The Germans took Brussels – which was declared an open city and thus suffered no destruction – on 20 August 1914. At first a similar fate was the lot of the ancient medieval university city of Louvain – 'the Oxford of Belgium'. However, claiming that some of their troops had been fired upon by *francs-tireurs* (guerrillas), thereby breaking the rules of war, German troops took revenge on 25 August 1914 by shelling a number of buildings including the historic church and the Clothworkers' Hall, a masterpiece of Gothic architecture. The university library – founded in 1426 and containing 230,000 volumes, including 750 priceless medieval illuminated manuscripts and 1000 of the earliest printed books – was also destroyed and looted in what was seen as 'The Sack of Louvain'. A similar fate then faced other cities as the advancing Germans began to implement a deliberate policy of *Schrecklichkeit* (Frightfulness) to terrorise the civilian population, in the hope that they would not resist and let them through to beat their real enemies, France and Britain, as soon as possible so that they could then turn and face the Russians on the Eastern Front.

Sullivan *(above right)* has the Kaiser's son, Crown Prince Wilhelm (heir to the throne of the Hohenzollern dynasty), literally dragging a sack marked 'Louvain' (out of which clocks and candlesticks can be seen projecting). He is wearing the uniform of his own regiment, the Death's Head Hussars, and is carrying a sword that has been transformed into a jemmy for prising open doors, cupboards and chests. In the other drawing by Sullivan *(below right)*, a crocodile (with a monkey in a *pickelhaube* helmet on its back) is shown wearing an Iron Cross (the German award for valour) as it devours a winged cherub and tramples on the cross of Jesus with its Latin acronym INRI (Jesus of Nazareth, King of the Jews). The Kaiser, who has a halo like the biblical saints, is dressed as Mr Pecksniff, the mean, hypocritical and treacherous character from Charles Dickens' *Martin Chuzzlewit*, who only forgives wrongdoing in himself and does the most heartless things 'as a duty to society'.

The Hope of the Hohenzollerns
'The Good German Sword'
Edmund J.Sullivan, *The Kaiser's Garland* (1915)

Crocodile Tears
Kaiser Pecksniff: **'My Heart Bleeds for Louvain'**
Edmund J. Sullivan, *The Kaiser's Garland* (1915)

The Gentle German
Edmund J.Sullivan, *The Kaiser's Garland* (1915)

The Prussian Butcher
Edmund J.Sullivan, *The Kaiser's Garland* (1915)

The Great German Civilisation
New 'Made in Germany' Streets for Belgian and French Villages Occupied by the German Army
Musini, *Numero* (Turin), 29 November 1914

The German policy of *Schrecklichkeit* continued during their advances deeper into Belgium. Allied propaganda spread many tales of babies being bayoneted, and children having their hands and women their breasts cut off. However, whatever the truth, atrocities did occur, and such was the wanton horror of this that it had the opposite effect and actually stiffened Belgian resistance. This in turn led to reprisals, amongst which was the shooting of 600 civilians (men, women and children) in the main square of Dinant on 23 August 1914, and the wanton destruction of artistic and architectural treasures. Such acts spawned what are known as 'hate' cartoons which are very far from being funny but are cartoons none the less. A number of examples are given here from Australia, France, Argentina, Italy and Britain.

**The Monster Advances –
The Advance of the Monster Must be Stopped**
Emilio Kupfer, *Critica* (Buenos Aires), 1915

'Don't be frightened, kill her – I've got hold of her.'
Francisque Poulbot, *L'Anti-Boche* (Paris) 1914

Australian poster, c.1914

Liberté! Liberté, Chérie!
Louis Raemaekers, 1914

For the Flag! For Victory!
French poster, 1917

And a Few Other Things
Napoleon said: 'Every soldier carries a field marshal's
baton in his knapsack.'
Bruce Bairnsfather, *Bystander*, 1915

The French, meanwhile – led by Commander-in-Chief General Joseph Joffre (with the backing of President Raymond Poincaré and Prime Minister René Viviani) – had been implementing their own pre-war strategy known as Plan 17 (it was the 17th annual revision). This proposed that in the event of a declaration of war with Germany, the French Army would launch an immediate attack into Alsace-Lorraine (lost during the Franco-Prussian War), aiming for the Rhine and then Berlin. They put this into operation in the first weeks of August 1914 but after a limited early success failed to make a major breakthrough. Then on 22 August 27,000 men were killed, making it the bloodiest day in French military history (dressed in old-fashioned red trousers and blue jackets the French soldiers made an easy target for German machine-gunners). As a result the offensive was called off, Plan 17 was abandoned and stalemate ensued.

The French war loan poster *(above right)* and the cartoon by Raemaekers *(above left)* display the *élan vital* (the vital spirit or will to win) that the French believed would carry their troops irresistibly forward in battle (led here by Marianne). The Raemaekers drawing also features the red trousers and soft képis which French soldiers wore into battle at the beginning of the war, whereas Bairnsfather's cartoon *(left)* of the more familiar steel-helmeted *poilu* (meaning 'shaggy') shows how their uniform changed after only a few months.

On 7 August 1914, soon after Britain declared war, the British Expeditionary Force of 100,000 men under the command of Field Marshal Sir John French was sent to France and, after arriving at Le Havre, took up its preordained station at Maubeuge, close to Mons on the French/Belgian border. As the Germans continued their sweep through Belgium, they were only held briefly by a heroic stand by members of the BEF. This was the first battle on European soil in which British troops had taken part since the Battle of Waterloo. The Kaiser ridiculed the BEF and commanded his generals to 'address all your skills and all the valour of my soldiers to exterminate first the treacherous English; walk over General French's contemptible little army.' However, the small, greatly outnumbered British force acquitted itself well in its first major action – being commended in particular for its rapid and accurate rifle fire – and its members thereafter proudly described themselves as 'The Old Contemptibles'. Even the Germans respected their stand and General Von Kluck said: 'At Mons the British taught the French how to die.' However, despite allegedly seeing 'the Angel of Mons' in the sky who protected their orderly retreat, the British troops soon joined the other Allies in full flight as the Germans swung southwest towards Paris as part of their Schlieffen Plan to encircle the capital and attack the French Army from behind.

With Paris now at risk and German troops only 20-odd miles away, the French commander of the capital, General Galliéni, spotted an exposed flank on a part of the German Army which had turned before reaching the city. Realising it was a unique opportunity, thousands of troops were sent across Paris by taxi to reach the front line and a major attack was launched on the Germans near the Marne River. This brilliant assault stopped the German advance in its tracks and effectively put paid to the Schlieffen Plan. The battle (which began on 6 September 1914) was later dubbed 'The Miracle of the Marne' and it marked a turning point of the war. From here on the two sides on the Western Front would have to resort to trench warfare.

Meanwhile, as the Battle of the Marne raged nearby, the Germans, in another apparent act of vandalism, shelled the ancient 13th-century Gothic French cathedral of Notre Dame in Rheims on 19 September 1914. Known as 'The Westminster Abbey of France' – as it was here that all the kings of France had been crowned from the 12th century to 1830 – this was deplored by the international community as much as the sacking of Louvain.

'The Hand of God' by Nelson Greene *(above right)* is one of the best known American cartoons of the war and was published in the weekly New York magazine *Puck*. The other drawing *(below right)* in which the cathedral has been rebuilt with artillery shells with the figure of death in the centre was published in the Dutch satirical weekly, *De Notenkraker* (The Nutcracker).

The Hand of God
Nelson Greene, *Puck*, 1914

Twentieth-Century Monumental Style
Albert Hahn, *De Notenkraker*, 26 September 1914

The Beer from the Spring Hops Has Arrived: The Enemy is Surrendering
Foldes, Hungarian poster, 1914

Meanwhile, on the Eastern Front, Austria-Hungary was faring badly. A number of attempted invasions of Serbia had been repulsed and early breakthroughs into Russian Poland had also been reversed. These four cartoons show opposing views of the situation.

In the Hungarian poster advertising a brand of beer *(left)*, German and Hungarian soldiers are shown leaning on a field gun and drinking beer which is so enticing that the enemy are seen surrendering *en masse* just so that they can join in. Amongst those with their hands up and holding a white flag of surrender are Scottish, English, Russian and Indian troops with (in the centre) a French soldier.

By contrast a Russian cartoon *(below right)* shows that, far from surrendering, even the Polish population are fighting back as a farm-girl skewers an Austrian soldier with her pitchfork, a view emphasised by the Polish drawing from *Mucha (below)*. The other Russian print *(above right)* has three vegetables – a potato, onion and a group of toadstools – transformed into Emperor Franz Joseph of Austria-Hungary, Kaiser Wilhelm of Germany and his son, the Crown Prince.

Austria is Astonished that Poles Should Assist Russia
Mucha (Warsaw), 1914

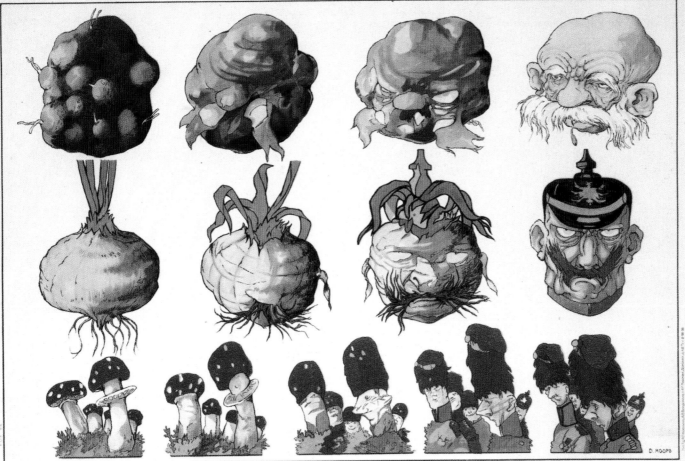

Russian print, 1914

Russian print, 1914

Retreat From the Front
Henri Armengol, *Le Rire Rouge* (Paris), 1914

The German in Belgium
Joe English, 1915

The Entrance of German Troops into Paris
Golia, *Numero* (Turin), 23 August 1914

After the Battle of the River Marne outside Paris, both sides began to dig trenches as a temporary measure. However, as time passed these got increasingly complex and ever more permanent. The Germans then began a 'Race to the Sea' with the Allies to try and outflank each other, with the added object of attempting to gain access to the important French ports of Dunkirk and Calais, thereby cutting off supplies of troops and weapons from Britain.

In the French cartoon *(top left)* German troops are depicted as hairs falling out of the Kaiser's head as they retreat from the Front, while the Italian drawing *(above)* from *Numero* (Italy was neutral at this stage of the war) implies that the only way the Germans will enter Paris is in chains. The Flemish cartoon *(top right)* by Joe English (1882-1918) was drawn in the trenches near the Yser Canal, which runs south from Nieuport on the Channel coast of Belgium. In the autumn of 1914, during the final stages of the 'Race to the Sea' the Belgian Army fought in the Battle of the Yser which culminated in King Albert ordering that the fields should be flooded, thereby finally halting the Germans who turned to concentrate their

Leo Cheney, Advertisement for Johnnie Walker Whisky,
December 1914

efforts against Ypres. The German soldier is saying to the Belgian widow, weeping at her husband's grave, 'But I still love you.'

Leo Cheney (1878-1928), who drew the last cartoon on this page *(bottom right)* was perhaps best known as the creator of the most famous version of the 'Johnnie Walker' character for the Scottish whisky brand.

By the end of October 1914 both sides had reached the coast but, as each had failed to outflank the other, they were forced to dig more trenches. These eventually stretched in a long double line – divided by a buffer zone known as No Man's Land – from the Swiss border to the North Sea coast, a distance of some 500 miles, with many supply trenches reaching backwards for miles on each side.

By then German troops occupied most of Belgium and the French industrial area (including all French coal supplies, all its iron fields and most of its heavy industry). In an attempt to break the deadlock the Germans launched an offensive in October 1914 to try and take the Belgian town of Ypres which was an important rail head for Allied troops and supplies from the French ports of Calais, Dunkirk and Boulogne.

However, by this time fresh British troops drawn from the Territorial Army (who were part-time soldiers in peacetime) had arrived to bolster the French and Belgian forces and the Germans suffered heavy casualties. At the First Battle of Ypres ('Wipers' to the British) 20,000 Germans were killed and 80,000 severely wounded during four weeks of intense fighting (the British lost 8000 and 40,000 wounded). On the allied side at Ypres was the cartoonist E.H.Shepard (later famous as the illustrator of A.A.Milne's 'Winnie the Pooh'), who won a Military Cross and achieved the rank of major. One of those fighting with the German troops was Corporal Adolf Hitler. (Hitler also saw action at the battles of Arras, the Somme, Neuve Chapelle – where he was wounded in the leg – and the Third Battle of Ypres, where he was gassed. He was awarded an Iron Cross, 1st Class, in 1918.)

Walker's British bulldog *(below)*, with its feet in Belgium and France has just eaten a plate of reinforcements and is ready for battle (Sam Weller said 'she's a swellin' wisibly before my wery eyes' in Dickens' *Pickwick Papers*).

In the cartoon *(top right)* by the Welshman Bert Thomas (1883-1966) – one of the most famous drawings of the war – an old hand pauses to light his pipe before going back into the fray. Reputedly sketched in ten minutes, it was first published on 11 November 1914 for a tobacco-for-the-troops appeal in the *Weekly Dispatch* but was later widely reprinted in many forms. A private in the Artists Rifles, Thomas was awarded an MBE in 1918.

A similar cartoon *(bottom right)* was produced as a postcard for Austria – Hungary when Italy entered the war on the side of the Allies in 1915.

' 'Arf a Mo', Kaiser!'
Bert Thomas, *Weekly Dispatch*, 11 November 1914

'Swelling Wisibly'
Reinforced Bulldog: **'NOW, where's that cultured Dachshund?'**
Jack Walker, *The Daily Graphic Special War Cartoons, No 4* (1914)

Hungarian postcard, n.d.

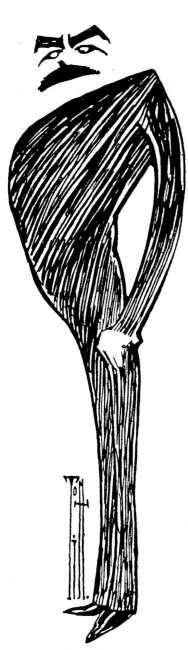

Lord Kitchener
Tom Titt, *Caricatures by Tom Titt* (1913)

Alfred Leete, poster, 1914

By September 1914 the BEF were suffering major casualties on the Western Front and fresh troops were needed. As Britain did not have conscription at that time (the only country in Europe which did not), the British War Secretary Lord Kitchener (the hero of Khartoum) asked at first for a further 100,000 volunteers to join what was left of the BEF's regular army troops. However, such was the degree of British patriotism that huge numbers applied – 500,000 in the first month and 100,000 a month for the next 18 months – and many had to be turned away at first.

The poster *(opposite)* of Lord Kitchener by Alfred Leete (1882-1933) is based on his earlier drawing for the cover of *London Opinion* magazine for 5 September 1914, but it has an additional strapline, as Kitchener insisted that all advertising for the Army should end with the words 'God Save the King'. The design was later copied by James Montgomery Flagg for a similar government poster campaign in the USA with Uncle Sam replacing Kitchener.

The well-known colour poster *(left)* by Savile Lumley (fl.1896-1949) is typical of the those used in the British government propaganda campaign to encourage men to join the armed forces.

'Daddy, What Did <u>You</u> Do in the Great War?'
Savile Lumley, poster, c.1915

Mooring a Dreadnought
E.G.O.Beuttler, *The Merry Mariners* (1917)

At sea the Royal Navy was the most powerful force in the world with more than 500 vessels at the beginning of the war. Pride of place amongst its warships was the huge 'Dreadnought' class of all-big-gun battleships. First introduced in December 1906 the original HMS *Dreadnought* was a revolutionary design and outclassed all other ships until the Orion class of 'Superdreadnoughts' were introduced in 1910. One of the navy's most important functions was to prevent supplies of food and war materiel getting to Germany. Its blockade of German ports was so successful that Germany lost one in four of its merchant ships to the British (Germany lost 41 ships in one day on 8 August 1914).

Amongst other measures designed to break the blockade the German navy chief, Admiral von Tirpitz, ordered the laying of mines, and the first naval action of the war was when the Royal Navy's light cruiser HMS *Amphion* was sunk by mines on 6 August 1914 with the loss of 100 lives (the British battleship HMS *Audacious* was also sunk by a mine on 27 October 1914). In a more direct encounter, the British Navy triumphed over the German High Seas Fleet at the Battle of Heligoland Bight (off the north German coast near Denmark) in August 1914, sinking four German ships and damaging three others. Meanwhile, the English coastal towns of Yarmouth (3 November 1914) and later Scarborough, Whitby and Hartlepool (16 December), were shelled by German cruisers, leaving a number of civilians killed or wounded. This was the first time enemy warships had killed anyone on the British mainland for more than a century (and the first time Scarborough had been attacked from the sea

Auckland Observer, 1914

The Tirpitz Touch
Cultured Skipper:
'And in the morning there will be/Another German victor-ee!'
Jack Walker, *The Daily Graphic Special War Cartoons, No.1* (1914)

since Harald Hardrada in 1066). In the Battle of Coronel (1 November) in the Pacific off Chile, Britain lost two cruisers to Admiral Von Spee's warships *Gneisenau* and *Scharnhorst*, but got its revenge at the Battle of the Falklands (8 December) when the German force (including the cruiser *Leipzig*) was sunk.

The cartoon *(opposite left)* by Edward Beuttler (1880-1964) – himself a lieutenant in the Royal Navy – shows the huge size of the Dreadnoughts and Superdreadnoughts and comes from his 1917 collection of cartoons, *The Merry Mariners*. Meanwhile, in the New Zealand cartoon *(opposite below left)* – which comments on the widespread use of seaborne mines by the Germans to close shipping lanes in the North Sea – the figure of Britannia prepares to attack a giant Kaiser who is seen planting these explosive seeds of destruction. Raemaekers' Dutch drawing *(right)* alludes to the fact that the German award for valour, the Iron Cross, seemed to be given out to all and sundry, while the Polish cartoon *(below right)* has the Kaiser having nightmares about his three lost cruisers.

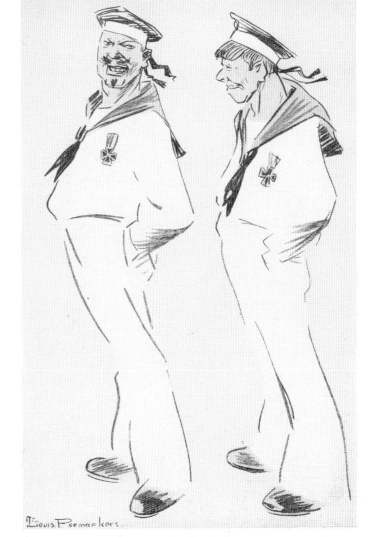

The Raid
'Do you remember Black Mary of Hamburg?'
'Aye, well.'
'She got six years for killing a child, whilst we get the Iron Cross for killing twenty at Hartlepool.'
Louis Raemaekers, 1914

The Heligoland 'Bight'
Jack Walker, *The Daily Graphic Special War Cartoons, No.1* (1914)

William's Nightmare
The Ghosts of His Lost Cruisers
Mucha (Warsaw), 1914

**The Influence of the Eagle on the Crescent
has Lately Become Evident**
Jack Walker, *The Daily Graphic Special War Cartoons, No. 4* (1914)

His Place in the Shade
The Man in the Moon: 'That sun was too hot!
I must be content with a crescent and a star.'
Jack Walker, *The Daily Graphic Special War Cartoons, No. 3* (1914)

Japan Joins in the Fight Against the Barbarians
French poster, 1914

As battle raged in Europe, war between the Allies and the Central Powers continued elsewhere in the world. Japan joined the Allies and declared war on Germany on 23 August 1914, and on 29 October Turkey joined the Central Powers, thereby widening their own sphere of influence in Asia.

Japan's first action was to attack Germany's main port in the Pacific, at Tsingtao in the district of Kiaochow in Shantung on the east coast of China facing Japan. Kiaochow had been leased to Germany for 99 years in 1898 and the port of Tsingtao had been built up into a major German naval base since then, providing the key to northern China and harbouring Admiral Von Spee's East Asia Squadron. The Japanese attack (aided by British troops) was a resounding success and Tsingtao, by then Germany's last base in the Pacific was taken on 7 November 1914 with 2500 prisoners.

The French poster *(above)* shows Japan as a fish, to symbolise that after Japan joined the Allies its main contribution was its navy, which provided protection for Allied convoys in the Far East and also escorted troopships in the Mediterranean from mid-1917.

Meanwhile, Jack Walker's two cartoons *(opposite, top)* show Germany's relations with her new ally, Turkey. In the left-hand drawing Japan is seen as the rising sun (the emblem of its flag) while the scorched Kaiser sits on the crescent moon labelled 'Turkey' and with the face of Sultan Mehmet V (Turkey's flag is a crescent moon and a star). On the right the Sultan's face is seen transforming into that of the Kaiser. (The phrase 'a place in the sun' was originally used by Count von Bülow, German Foreign Secretary and later Bethmann-Hollweg's predecessor as Chancellor, in the Reichstag on 6 December 1897 to refer to East Asia: 'In a word, we desire to throw no one into the shade, but we also demand our own place in the sun'.)

The French drawing *(right)* makes fun of Germany's decrepit allies, while the opposite view is taken by the cartoons from *Meggendorfer-Blätter* and *Simplicissimus (below)* – the latter featuring a British soldier having to share a meal with other allied prisoners.

Wilhelm: 'And me too, I've got allies!'
Maurice Radiguet, *Le Rire* (Paris), 5 December 1914

The Triple Entente
Meggendorfer-Blätter, 1915

The Gentleman Amongst the Prisoners:
'What Barbarians! Fancy having to eat with our Allies.'
Simplicissimus (Munich), 1914

The Ungartered Blackleg
(Honi soit...)
Edmund J.Sullivan, *The Kaiser's Garland* (1915)

HRH Prince Louis of Battenberg
Tom Titt (Jan Stanislaw de Junosza Rosciszewski),
Caricatures (1913)

The Rape of the Germans in England
Arthur Johnson, 1914

There was a lot of anti-German feeling in Britain after the outbreak of war, especially after the shelling of the East Coast and reports of atrocities in Belgium. Many shops which had Teutonic-sounding names were attacked and looted and Germans or Austrians who had become naturalised British citizens – many of them working as musicians (especially in brass bands), children's governesses or barbers – were treated with suspicion as possible spies and many were interned in prison camps on the Isle of Man and elsewhere. (Even the dachshund breed of dog died out in the UK and had to be reintroduced after the war.) This reached such a pitch by October 1914 that the Austrian-born Prince Louis of Battenberg (grandson of Louis II of Hesse) – who had been First Sea Lord since 1912 – resigned his post at the end of the month (being replaced by 'Jacky' Fisher), despite the fact that by then both his brother Prince Henry and his nephew Prince Maurice had died for Britain in the war.

The British royal family also later changed its name from Saxe-Coburg-Gotha to Windsor, rejected all its German titles and honours and stripped the Kaiser of membership of the select Order of the Garter (its French motto was *Honi soit qui mal y pense* – evil be to him who thinks evil) and other British honours. As an additional mark of patriotism Prince Albert (the future George VI) served in the Royal Navy and the Prince of Wales (later Edward VIII) was appointed to Sir John French's staff in France. (Britain was not alone in its anti-German stance – in Russia there was so much anti-German feeling that on 1 September 1914 its capital St Petersburg was renamed Petrograd.)

The drawing by Sullivan *(opposite)* shows George V taking away the Kaiser's garter – to reveal a hairy demonic leg (a 'blackleg' is also a turncoat) – throwing down the star that denotes the exclusive Order of the Garter and breaking his ceremonial sword. Johnson's German cartoon*(above right)*, by contrast, points out that as the King himself is German by descent, both from Queen Victoria's Hanoverian forebears and more directly from her German husband Prince Albert, he too should be interned in a concentration camp.

Russian postcard, 1914

Though the Russians had lost 125,000 men to the German Army at the Battle of the Masurian Lakes (9-10 September) they had better success against the Austro-Hungarian forces in Poland. On 11 September 1914 they captured the fortress of Lemberg (now known as Lvov), in Galicia, and before long also began to have some success against the Germans, notably stopping a major offensive by Hindenburg outside Warsaw and making a successful counterattack at Lodz.

The first of these two patriotic Russian *lubok* prints *(left)* shows Tsar Nicholas thrashing a German, while in the second *(above)* Russian troops are imagined as besieging Berlin. In the background can be seen the Eiffel Tower and the caption implies that by the time the Germans get to Paris, the Russians will have taken Berlin.

The drawing of the Kaiser in the form of a cat *(right)* is a direct reference to the famous eighteenth-century Russian print of the Kazan Cat which itself satirised the autocratic Peter the Great of Russia.

Russian postcard, 1914

Russian print, n.d.

Study of a Prussian Household Having its Morning Hate
Frank Reynolds, *Punch*, 24 February 1915

The Hymn of Hate
'A Little Bit of Sugar for the Bird'
Edmund J.Sullivan, *The Kaiser's Garland* (1915)

The Gnashing Room in a Berlin Hate Club
Leo Cheney, *Bystander*, 14 April 1915

The 'Hymn of Hate Against England' *'Hassgesang Gegen England'* was written by a German-Jewish poet called Ernst Lissauer (1882-1937), a friend of Stefan Zweig, in August 1914. Very popular amongst Germans, its refrain was:

> We love as one, we hate as one,
> We have one foe and one alone –
> ENGLAND!

The complete text of the song was published (in English) in Britain in the *Weekly Dispatch* (with a musical setting) and *The Times* (October 1914) and many German publications ran articles entitled *'Unser Hass Gegen England'* (Our Hatred of England). Kaiser Wilhelm later presented Lissauer with the Order of the Red Eagle, 4th Class. The 'Hymn of Hate' became one of most popular songs in Germany during the war.

Sullivan's cartoon *(above right)* has the Kaiser giving a sugar cube to Ernst Lissauer who is drawn as a freely roaming German parrot – note the Order of the Red Eagle – as they sing the hymn of hate together, while two love-birds (marked 'Dangerous') sit trapped in a small cage below.

The *Punch* cartoon *(above left)* by Frank Reynolds (1876-1953) is one of the best known cartoons of the Great War. Reynolds was art editor of *Punch* from 1920 to 1930. A similar sentiment is shown in the drawing by Leo Cheney *(left)*. Note the phrase *Gott Strafe England* on the beersteins, above the door and even on the waiter's cuffs, while the phonograph plays a record of the song *The Hymn of Hate*.

Teutonic Barber: 'Shafe, sir?'
Customer: 'Ye-es – that is, no! – I think I'll try a haircut.'
F.H.Townsend, *Punch*, 16 September 1914

Alfred Leete, cover, *Schmidt the Spy and His Messages to Berlin* (1915)

Anti-German feeling in Britain reached its high point when it was discovered that Gustav Steinhauer, the head of the German secret service, had set up a spy-ring run from a barber's shop on the Caledonian Road in Islington, London. One German agent, Gustav Müller, even communicated using advertisements in the personal columns of the *Daily Telegraph*. In all 21 German spies were sentenced to death in Britain in the Great War, of which 14 were executed and 7 had their convictions commuted to imprisonment. Other countries also executed spies, a notable example being that of the Dutch exotic dancer Mata Hari (Margaretha Geertruida Zelle) who was shot by the French in Vincennes in 1917.

The cartoon *(right)* by Claude Shepperson (1867-1921), alludes to the fact that many children's governesses in upper-class British households before the war were German, while Townsend's *(above left)* harks back to the days of Sweeney Todd, 'the demon barber of Fleet Street'. Schmidt the Spy *(above right)* was created for *London Opinion* magazine by Alfred Leete (1882-1933) – who also drew the famous Kitchener recruiting poster – and his exploits were later collected into a book, whose cover is shown here. Indeed, so popular was the Schmidt character that in April 1916 he starred in a live-action film made by Phoenix Films with Lewis Sydney playing the part of the spy.

Ethel (in apprehensive whisper which easily reaches her German governess, to whom she is deeply attached): 'Mother, shall we have to kill Fräulein?'
Claude Shepperson, *Punch*, 2 September 1914

He is to Blame
German poster, c.1914

Wollt ihr dieses?
so meldet Euch zum Freiwilligen (II.) Garde Grenadier Batl.

Spandau: Neue Kaserne, Schmidt Knobelsdorffstraße

Schützt Euer Land

Would You Like to Keep This?
German recruiting poster, Berlin, c.1914

Many intelligent Germans – even literary figures like the playwright Gerhard Hauptmann – claimed that Britain had 'conspired to bring about this war'. In a speech to the Reichstag on 2 December 1914, the German Chancellor Theobald von Bethmann-Hollweg officially blamed England for the war (he made no distinction between England and Great Britain as a whole). This gave added force to the popular German catchphrase *'Gott Strafe England'* (May God Punish England) with its response *'Er Strafe Es'* (He Will Punish Her).

The stark German propaganda poster on the left shows an evil-looking British soldier and British bulldog and asserts that the war is their fault. By contrast the one on the right with its peaceful view of German village life asks a pertinent question. Naturally assuming the answer to be 'Yes' the text then suggests that to do so the reader should enlist in the Grenadier Guards Battalion in Spandau.

The poster *(opposite)* entitled 'Aid for the Victims of War' – was drawn by Leonid Pasternak, father of the future Nobel Prize-winning Russian writer Boris Pasternak (author of *Doctor Zhivago*). Produced shortly after the outbreak of war, the image was a huge success and was later reproduced on postcards, sweet wrappers and labels and was even featured in the British journal, *Studio*.

The Wounded Soldier
Leonid O.Pasternak, Russian aid poster, 1914

When WILLIAM comes with all his might
And sets the river Thames alight,
I shouldn't be at all surprised
If London Town were Teutonised.

Bidding his bands to play *Te Deum*
He'll occupy the Athenæum,
And Pallas' Owl become a vulture
Under the new *régime* of culture.

Britons will have to pay a mark
For leave to sit inside the Park

And watch the noble Uhlans go
Careering up and down the Row.

In this imaginative 'What If?' fancy by Townsend in *Punch*, the Kaiser is seen mounting the steps of the exclusive Athenaeum Club in Pall Mall on a horse while a German brass band plays the *Te Deum* (a Latin hymn so called after its opening words '*Te Deum Laudamus*' – Thee God We Praise). Then in the second picture Britons have to pay a Deutschmark each to sit in Hyde Park at Hyde Park Corner while Uhlans ride by (the Uhlans were an elite German cavalry corps) – note that the woman talking to the senior officer is meant to be German as she has two dachshunds. In the third picture an overweight Kaiser dressed in the uniform of a Death's Head Hussar (the Crown Prince's regiment) leads a troop of overweight German dancing girls in song while holding beersteins and a sausage. The final frame is set in the dining-room of the Savoy Hotel, London – renamed the Saveloy after the famous sausage. (Note the young British waiter being brushed aside by the pompous Germans arriving down the steps.)

A higher Art will mould our tastes
To Teuton wit and Teuton waists;

And when their houris ply the hoof
The house will rock from floor to roof.

On Pilsen beer the Bosch will bloat,
Supplied by Herren APPENRODT,

And German sausage be his joy
At the new-christened Saveloy.

When William Comes to London
F.H.Townsend, *Punch Almanack for 1915* (1914)

Men of Few Words
Grand Duke Nicholas: 'Ça marche?'
General Joffre: 'Assez bien. Et chez vous?'
Grand Duke: 'Pas mal.'
F.H.Townsend, *Punch*, 2 December 1914

By the end of 1914 the Entente Allies could look back on a reasonably successful year on all fronts and look forward to a major new offensive in the spring of 1915 – to be bolstered by the arrival of large numbers of fresh British troops from Kitchener's New Army. Germany's outlook was less optimistic. It had lost all its colonies in the Pacific, had been held by France and Britain in the West, and – despite a huge defeat at Tannenberg in East Prussia – Russia continued to hold both German and Austro-Hungarian forces at bay in the East.

In Townsend's cartoon from December 1914 Grand Duke Nicholas (the Tsar's uncle and Commander-in-Chief of the Russian Army) telephones General Joseph Joffre (Commander-in-Chief of the French Army and leader of the Allied forces in the west), the telephone wire itself linking and framing the two panels. The French text reads: 'How is it going?' 'Well enough, and what about your end?' 'Not bad.' (It should be remembered that long-distance telephony and portable handsets like those shown were new in 1914 – indeed the telephone itself had only been invented 40 years earlier.)

His Dual Obsession
Owing to the frequent recurrence of this dream, Herr Fritz von Lagershifter has decided to take his friends' advice: Give up sausage late at night and brood less upon the possible size of the British Army next spring.
Bruce Bairnsfather, *Bystander*, 1915

British greetings card, 1917

Bruce Bairnsfather, Christmas 1914

However, the troops on the ground took a different view as they faced their first Christmas in the trenches. One result of this was the so-called Christmas Truce when Germans and British broke all the rules of war and fraternised with the enemy, playing football in No Man's Land, singing 'Silent Night' and other Christmas songs together and swapping food, wine and cigarettes. The British cartoonist Bruce Bairnsfather was present at one section of the front where this happened. 'I spotted a German officer...and being a bit of a collector, I intimated to him that I had taken a fancy to some of his buttons. We both said things to each other which neither understood, and agreed to do a swap. I brought out my wire clippers and, with a few deft snips, removed a couple of his buttons and put them in my pocket. I then gave him two of mine in exchange.' Also shown *(top right)* is a greetings card produced for the British 11th Division for Christmas and New Year 1917/18.

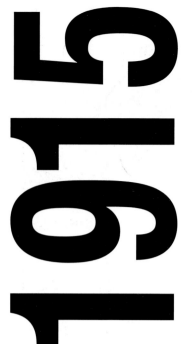

1915

THE STALEMATE on the Western Front continued in 1915 as trench warfare became the norm. Each side tried to break the deadlock by major offensives in France and Belgium at Neuve Chapelle, Ypres, Artois and elsewhere, but the cost in human lives began to soar, especially when faced with such devastating modern technology as machine-guns, poison gas, flame-throwers, fighter aircraft and enormous long-range guns developed by the German company of Krupp.

With the entry of Italy into war on the side of the Allies in May, there was hope that the tide would turn. However, this was quickly dashed by Italian defeats at the first of many battles of the Isonzo, the entry of Bulgaria into the conflict on the side of the Central Powers in October, and the final defeat of Serbia by Austro-Hungarian and Bulgarian forces the following month.

Meanwhile, on the Eastern Front the Russians also fared badly. Despite successfully capturing the heavily fortified Austro-Hungarian garrison at Przemysl in the Carpathians (seen as the key to Hungary) in March, they soon found themselves under such heavy attack from the combined might of Germany and Austria-Hungary, that they were forced to give it up and within a few months had retreated 300 miles to Warsaw, losing a million men as prisoners and much of modern Poland, Belarus, the Ukraine and Lithuania. This disaster led to the sacking of Grand Duke Nicholas as head of the Russian armed forces and his replacement by Tsar Nicholas II himself.

To give some relief to Russia the other Allies launched an offensive in the Dardanelles in an attempt to take Constantinople (modern Istanbul) and knock Turkey out of the war. However, after initial success, the Gallipoli campaign – the largest amphibious assault ever, until D-Day in World War II – also went badly wrong and the Allied forces had to be evacuated. Another Allied setback came after an attempt to take Turkish-held Baghdad ended with defeat at Kut where 12,000 British and Indian troops were taken prisoner after a long siege.

At sea things also looked bleak. In an effort to starve out Britain, Germany began unrestricted submarine warfare against all shipping, neutral or otherwise. This led to the sinking of the British civilian transatlantic cruise liner *Lusitania* – the world's largest and most luxurious liner – off the coast of Ireland with great loss of life. Other human tragedies this year included the deportation and massacre of 800,000 Armenians by the Turks.

In December 1914 the British had declared Egypt a protectorate and started to move troops into the area around the Suez Canal, Britain's link from the Mediterranean to its Empire in India, Australia and New Zealand, as well as the oil-producing Gulf states. In February 1915, 20,000 Turkish troops based in Ottoman-held Palestine marched 150 miles through the Sinai Desert to try and capture the Suez Canal. Indian troops commanded by British officers not only repelled the attack but also began themselves to advance into Palestine, with the aim of taking Jerusalem.

The cartoon by Edwin Morrow *(right)* may possibly be one of the first ever jokes about modern German tourists. *Bier fur Hoching* means 'beer for saying *hoch*' (similar to 'three cheers' and used as a salute to the Kaiser, not unlike 'Heil Hitler' in World War II), and a number of men can be seen raising their beermugs at the left of the picture. Meanwhile, the German cartoon *(below left)* has Lord Kitchener as a nonchalant Achilles filling his pipe with one foot on the Sphinx, unaware of the German shooting an arrow over Turkey and into his heel (Egypt), traditionally his weakest point. The verse which originally appeared under this drawing can be translated as 'Hit him there and hit him hard;/And English blood will give the sands a feast./So draw the bow and be on guard;/Ready to kill the English – through the East.'

In Egypt – Not Yet!
Awful Prospect in Egypt If and When the Germans Come
Edwin Morrow, *Bystander*, 3 February 1915

German cartoon, 1915

Suez-Side!
Jack Walker, *The Daily Graphic Special War Cartoons, No. 6* (1915)

An amusing view of the main leaders of the Central Powers depicted as circus performers. The cards Bethmann-Hollweg (German Chancellor 1909-17) is displaying are ration cards and the reference to nails in the portrait of General Hindenburg not only alludes to his 'hard-as-nails' tough-man image but also to the fact that wooden statues of him were erected all over Germany into which members of the public were invited to hammer a nail as a way of raising funds for the war effort. The 'Veteran Tyrolese Jodeler' is Emperor Franz Joseph I of Austria-Hungary, 'Fearless Ferdie' is King Ferdinand of Bulgaria (which joined the Central Powers in 1915), 'Little Willie' is Crown Prince Wilhelm of Germany and 'Weary Mehmed' is Sultan Mehmet V of the Ottoman Empire (note the tattered clothes indicating that the Ottoman Empire is on its last legs). 'Tino' is King Constantine I of Greece who is shown trying to balance on a high wire to suggest that though pro-German (his wife was the Kaiser's sister) he had not yet officially committed his country to either side (he was later deposed and Greece joined the Allies).

Bernard Partridge (1861-1945) – who was knighted in 1925 – succeeded Linley Sambourne as *Punch*'s main artist in 1910 and continued to produce the magazine's main political drawings through the Great War and right up till his death during World War II.

58

The Potsdam Variety Troupe
Bernard Partridge, *Punch's Almanack for 1917*, December 1916

The Paper Boat
Jack Walker, *The Daily Graphic Special War Cartoons, No. 6* (1915)

The Sea Serpent is Generally Considered a Myth
Jack Walker, *The Daily Graphic Special War Cartoons, No. 6* (1915)

Having been successfully blockaded by the Royal Navy since the beginning of the war, Germany decided not to risk its capital ships in a major shoot-out for the foreseeable future and concentrated instead on a submarine blockade of Britain to try and starve the country out. In consequence, on 18 February 1915, Admiral Tirpitz declared that Germany would conduct unrestricted submarine warfare against all shipping, neutral or otherwise, which tried to supply food and armaments to the UK. The two cartoons *(above)* by

Jack Walker of the *Daily Graphic* make fun of Germany's blockade (note that the letters on the U-boat serpent spell 'Blockade'), while in Lunt's poster *(below left)* the 'pirates and pledge-breakers' are Hindenburg, the Kaiser, Crown Prince Wilhelm and Von Tirpitz. The German cartoon *(below right)* refers to recent naval losses by the Allies – HMS *Majestic* was torpedoed off Gallipoli, HMS *Formidable* was torpedoed in the English Channel and the French battleship *Le Bouvet* was sunk by mines in the Dardanelles.

Wilmot Lunt, British poster, 1915

King George and M. Poincaré Hold a Naval Review
German cartoon, c.July 1915

As part of this new U-boat strategy, on 30 April 1915 the German Embassy in New York took out an advertisement in US newspapers threatening that the Imperial German Navy would sink the British Cunard Line cruise ship *Lusitania* if it left New York for its usual transatlantic destination, Liverpool. (The *Lusitania* had earlier beaten its German rival to win the famous Blue Riband award for the fastest crossing of the Atlantic.) Undeterred, the ship set sail and as a result on 7 May was sunk off the southwest coast of Ireland by a German submarine (U-20) – 1198 were drowned including 124 US citizens. There was such widespread condemnation of this action – especially from neutral USA – that Germany called off its unrestricted warfare campaign for two years. Many expected this incident to drag the USA into the war on the side of the Allies but instead, on 10 May 1915 President Wilson announced in an address to foreign-born citizens of the USA: 'There is such a thing as a man being too proud to fight.' Germany felt it had given due warning of its intent to sink the ship – which was also carrying 173 tons of rifle ammunition – and added insult to injury by striking a medal to commemorate the sinking of the *Lusitania*.

The German and French cartoons *(right)* take a cynical view on the drowning of US citizens travelling on British ships.

The Valuable Cargo
'All right men, the old lady with the blue glasses is an American.
Nobody save her by mistake if we're torpedoed.'
Simplicissimus (Munich), 25 April 1916

You Can Torpedo This Ship, It Has No Americans – Uncle Sam
'Now I see why these gentlemen are waiting for me!'
Jules Grandjouan, *Le Rire* (Paris), 31 July 1915

Henri Lanos, *Le Rire Rouge,* 27 March 1915

In early 1915 the Russian Army faced new assaults from the south when the Turkish Navy attacked the Black Sea ports of Odessa and Sebastopol and the Turkish Army began an offensive in the Caucasus. In consequence they appealed to the other Allies for a diversionary campaign to take the pressure off them. This took the form of the Dardanelles Offensive, supported by First Sea Lord Winston Churchill, which was both designed to capture Constantinople (Istanbul) – and thereby knock Turkey out of the war – and also to encourage the then neutral Balkan countries to join the Allied cause.

However, the Dardanelles Offensive did not go according to plan. The campaign began when French and British warships bombarded Turkish forts along the narrow waterway between the Mediterranean and the Black Sea. It soon became evident that naval power alone was insufficient to break through the straits – which were heavily protected by mines, nets and gun batteries – and three ships were sunk by mines and three more damaged. In consequence the Allies withdrew and planned instead an overland amphibious attack on Constantinople via the Gallipoli peninsula. (In the build-up to the invasion, British poet Rupert Brooke died of blood poisoning from a mosquito bite in a hospital ship moored off the Greek island of Skyros. It is ironic that the poet actually died at sea, having earlier written the famous lines: 'If I should die, think only this of me:/ that there's some corner of a foreign field/ that is forever England'.)

By the Waters of the Dardanelles We Sat Down and Wept
German cartoon, 1915

The Battle of Gallipoli – which took place near the ancient site of Troy – was at that time the greatest seaborne invasion ever. On 25 April 1915, an initial assault of 30,000 British, French, Australian and New Zealand troops under General Sir Ian Hamilton landed on the Gallipoli peninsula. However, many of the Allied soldiers soon became pinned down on the beaches and faced stiff resistance from Turkish troops, including a number of successful counterattacks by Mustapha Kemal (who was seen as a Turkish hero and later became leader of Turkey under the name Kemal Attaturk). The situation later led to stagnation and General Hamilton was replaced by General Sir Charles Munro in October. After nine months of intense fighting and huge casualties on both sides (205,000 British Empire and 47,000 French dead, wounded or missing) the Allies pulled out of Gallipoli on 20 December 1915. The failure of the Dardanelles campaign – which was celebrated as a tremendous victory by the Turks – also led to the replacement of Winston Churchill as First Sea Lord.

In the Russian cartoon *(above right)* a Russian cavalryman shakes his fist at a group of Turkish men as ships pass through the Dardanelles. Meanwhile, in the French drawing *(above left)*, a military boot kicks over a box of Turkish fez hats (labelled 'Made in Germany') as Allied warships approach the coast of Asia on the eastern side of Dardanelles. Not surprisingly, the German cartoon *(below left)* makes much of the failure of the initial attack with France and Britain repairing their broken ships while Turkey looks on. The allusion in the title is to the Biblical lament 'By the waters of Babylon we sat down and wept.'

The Dardanelles Offensive was also the first major conflict in which the Australian and New Zealand forces had taken part in large numbers, something that is shown in this Australian recruiting poster.

Russian postcard, c.1915

A Call From the Dardanelles
Australian recruiting poster, 1915

The Reign of Officialdom
The Official (to DORA): **'Go and see what the British public is doing
– and tell it not to.'**
Wilton Williams, *London Opinion*, 16 March 1918

No Joke!
*The Censor has been most kind to me throughout the war. I have made the
above drawing simply out of gratitude. I have also omitted the joke, thus
ensuring complete approval.*
Bruce Bairnsfather, *Bystander*, 1916

Lack of information about what was actually happening in the war
was frustrating for civilians on both sides of the conflict. Censorship
had been introduced in Britain at an early stage by the Defence of the
Realm Act (DORA) – with its many intrusive restrictions – which
became law on 8 August 1914. In 1915 the British Socialist paper
Forward was banned after it reported that 3000 shop stewards in
Glasgow had refused to hear Lloyd George speak and the London
Globe – the oldest evening paper in Britain at the time – was also
suspended by the government on 16 November 1915 for publishing
misleading statements about Lord Kitchener.

On the right can be seen a spoof cover of the 3880th issue of
Punch which was produced for the 1916 *Almanack*. Supposedly
censored as fit for German consumption, it is a direct parody of the
famous Richard Doyle cover first published in 1849 and features the
Kaiser in the place of Mr Punch, a dachshund instead of Toby the
dog, Crown Prince William as Mr Punch on an ass in the lower frieze,
and numerous Germanic references including sausages, Zeppelins
and Hydrogen Chloride poison gas (under the chair). John Bull at
the top is seen as being 'in the soup' and the British lion on the easel
has his tail between his legs.

NOTE.—THIS ISSUE OF "PUNCH," HAVING BEEN IMPERIALLY CENSORED AND
REFINED, IS NOW PASSED AS FIT FOR GERMAN AND NEUTRAL CONSUMPTION.

THE ABOVE DESIGN HAS BEEN APPROVED BY THE IMPERIAL GERMAN CENSOR, CERTAIN
MODIFICATIONS OF THE ORIGINAL HAVING BEEN INTRODUCED BY
A HUMOURIST OF THE FATHERLAND.

F.H.Townsend, *Punch Almanack for 1916*, December 1915

Russian print, c.1915

Freeing Poland from Russian's Yoke
Der Wahre Jacob (Stuttgart), 17 September 1915

The German victories at Tannenberg and at the Masurian Lakes in East Prussia in the autumn of 1914 led to considerable civil unrest in Russia with conscription riots and strikes. In an effort to calm the population the government revoked its ban of the production and sale of vodka (introduced in August 1914) and recalled the Duma (Parliament) to take other measures to strengthen morale. As a result, when a German offensive was launched towards Warsaw in January 1915 the Russians not only withstood the assault but also mounted a successful counterattack. In addition they had considerable success against Austria-Hungary in Galicia which resulted in the taking of the strategically important fortress city of Przemysl which held the key to Hungary. Przemysl had been shelled by the Russians for six months and 300 defenders a day died of starvation in the fortress. In a final assault in March 1915 the fortress was captured and 126,000 prisoners – including nine generals and 700 big guns – were taken. After this disastrous defeat the Germans said they were 'shackled to a corpse' (i.e. Austria-Hungary). A third of the population of Przemysl were Jewish and when the Russians took over they banned the Jews from owning shops.

Przemysl was recaptured by the Germans and Austro-Hungarians later in the year, in July Warsaw fell, and by the autumn the Russians had retreated 300 miles and been pushed out of Poland and the Austro-Hungarian region of Galicia. The Russian print *(above)* depicts the early triumphs over the Central Powers, while the German cartoon from *Lustige Blätter (below right)* satirises the Tsar (known as the Little Father as he was very short) and the Grand Duke Nicholas (the tall Russian Army chief) as they try and quell the rioting citizens of Petrograd by giving them back some vodka ('*Freiheit! Das russische Volk*' means 'Freedom! The Russian People'). The cover of *Der Wahre Jacob (above right)*, meanwhile, sees the German victory as liberation for the Poles (note the Russian bear running off through the woods and the knout beneath Germania's foot).

The Little Father Pacifies
Tsar: 'Above all, don't scream, my children! There! you shall have the bottle again.'
Lustige Blätter, 1915

The Russians also had considerable success against Turkey in 1915. In December Turkey launched an invasion through the Caucasus Mountains that bordered the two countries. However, they suffered terrible losses, with 25,000 poorly equipped men freezing to death before they even met the Russian forces. The Russian poster *(right)* shows a medieval Russian knight attacking a hydra-headed monster representing the Central Powers. As can be seen, he has already cut off the head of Austria-Hungary, has wounded Germany and is now about to attack Turkey. In the background on the left can be seen the ruins of Rheims cathedral.

The Great European War
Russian poster, c.1915

Hindenburg in Difficulties
'I intended to get my feet firmly in Russia and now it is Russia that has got *me* firmly by the feet!'
Il Travaso (Rome), 1915

The Poison Bombs
Humanity: 'Is there no limit to *Kultur*?'
Leo Cheney, *Daily Chronicle*, 1915

Thick Air
'Gas alarm! – No, don't worry, it's just the company in the next
trench smoking their Ersatz shrub tobacco!'
Simplicissimus (Munich), 1918

Ecce Homo
De Notenkraker, 13 April 1918

No 'Light' Call
'Bert, 'ere's the man about the gas.'
Bruce Bairnsfather, *Bystander*, 1916

'Fancy, how nice! They are drinking death in their sleep.'
Louis Raemaekers, 1915

The first use of chemical weapons in the Great War was at the Battle of Bolimov near Warsaw when the Germans used tear-gas against Russian troops but the wind blew it back onto their own troops. On 14 April 1915 the Germans accused the French of using poison gas near Verdun but the first major use was in the Second Battle of Ypres (22 April-25 May 1915). The Germans began the offensive using greenish-yellow chlorine gas on the Langemarck sector of the Ypres salient. The recipients were French and Algerian troops. Later Britain and France also used poison gas. At first the gas was launched from cylinders but later gas-filled shells fired from artillery were developed and new deadlier varieties such as phosgene and mustard gas were used.

Considerable psychological pressure was put on young men to join up and fight during the Great War. Those who did not enlist were classified as shirkers, and in Britain it became commonplace for elderly women to accost men of military age who were out of uniform and present them with white feathers as a sign of cowardice. The British government propaganda poster, as well as the *Punch* cartoon by Thomas Maybank *(overleaf)*, reflect the national mood at this time.

COVER FOR SHIRKERS.

It is daily requiring more and more courage for the man of military age not in uniform to be seen enjoying outdoor pleasures.

THE SUNDAY MORNING CONSTITUTIONAL.

THE JOY-RIDE.

TEA-TIME IN THE BACKWATER.

Cover for Shirkers
Thomas Maybank, *Punch*, 16 June 1915

Women of Britain say 'Go!'
British recruitment poster

Cheerful one (to newcomer, on being asked what the trenches are like): '**If yer stands up yer gets sniped; if yer keeps down yer gets drowned; if yer moves yer get shelled; and if yer stands still yer gets court-martialled for frost-bite.**'
Claude Shepperson, *Punch*, 26 January 1916

'There goes our blinkin' parapet again'
Bruce Bairnsfather, *Bystander*, 1915

The Fatalist
'**I'm sure they'll 'ear this damn thing squeakin'.'**
Bruce Bairnsfather, *Bystander*, 1915

The British are proud of their sense of humour, particularly in adversity, and the four cartoons shown here capture this very well. The 'Better 'Ole' cartoon is one of the most famous drawings of the Great War on either side of the conflict and made its artist internationally famous. It was drawn by Captain Bruce Bairnsfather, a machine-gun officer in the Royal Warwickshire Regiment. Fellow soldiers in Bairnsfather's battalion included Bernard Montgomery (who had already won a DSO and would become legendary in World War II) and A.A.Milne (later deputy editor of *Punch* and creator of 'Winnie the Pooh').

While stationed near Armentières on the Western Front in January 1915 Bairnsfather began to draw a series of cartoons which would later be called 'Fragments from France'. The first of these, 'Where did that one go to?' was published in the *Bystander* magazine in January 1915. Bairnsfather later served in the Second Battle of Ypres where he was injured by a shell blast and returned to England for hospital treatment. The 'Better 'Ole' cartoon was drawn after he had recovered and while he was working as machine-gun instructor at the headquarters of the 34th Division at Sutton Veney on Salisbury Plain, Wiltshire. It was a huge success and a collection of his *Bystander* cartoons, *Fragments From France* sold more than 250,000 copies in 1916 alone.

WELL, IF YOU KNOWS OF A BETTER 'OLE, GO TO IT!

One of Our Minor Wars
'Well if you knows of a better 'ole, go to it'
Bruce Bairnsfather, *Bystander*, 24 November 1915 (Christmas edition)

The Broken Alliance and Italy
'Twenty years and more you've forced me to wear this chain.'
Louis Raemaekers, 1915

Putting Him in His Place
Austrian Emperor: 'How well our arms are doing!'
German Emperor (coldly): 'Quite so. By the way, I hear you've
got a war on with Italy. Any news from that front?'
F.H.Townsend, *Punch*, 28 July 1915

Encouraged by the initial success of the Allies in the Dardanelles and promises of Austro-Hungarian lands agreed by the secret Pact of London (signed on 26 April 1915), Italy declared war on Austria-Hungary – with which it shared its northern border – on 23 May. (It declared war on Turkey on 20 August 1915 and on Germany on 28 August 1916.) For two years the Italian and Austro-Hungarian forces burrowed into the Alps, reflecting the trench warfare on the Western Front. However, the border levelled off at the Isonzo River and over the coming years there were eleven Battles of the Isonzo in which 300,000 Italians were killed.

In Townsend's cartoon *(above right)* the Kaiser puts down an over-optimistic Emperor Franz Joseph of Austria-Hungary, while the German drawing *(left)* has Asquith as John Bull teaching a parrot whose head-feathers resemble those in an Italian *Bersaglieri* military hat.

War Against Germany
'At last he has learnt his lesson. Now he shall be allowed to be fed.'
Simplicissimus (Munich), 1916

The one ally both Germany and the Entente Powers really wanted was the USA. This was long before the Anglo-US 'special relationship' and it is not easy in hindsight to realise that there was a lot of isolationism in the USA at this time – the war between the Allies and the Central Powers was seen as a purely European conflict and the USA could (and did) sell supplies to both sides. In addition, there was also a lot of pro-German feeling in the country as it had a large German population. In 1914 eight million Americans had German parents or grandparents and 4.5 million were of Irish descent and disliked Britain. Indeed, when war broke many thousands of Americans (and not just German Americans) volunteered to serve on the *German* side.

Townsend's *Punch* cartoon (which was published over a whole page of the magazine) sums up the expectations of Germany at this time, while Thomas's drawing *(below)* shows Britain's increasing frustration. In the German cartoon *(below right)* President Wilson sits astride the US financier, J.P.Morgan, on his pile of gold.

Nothing Doing
Imperial Dachshund: 'Here I've been sitting up and doing tricks for the best part of seven weeks, and you take no more notice of me than if –'
Uncle Sam: 'Cut it out!'
F.H.Townsend, *Punch*, 23 September 1914

The USA Note
John Bull: 'Sorry to inconvenience you, but if we don't get this fire out, your place will go next.'
Uncle Sam: 'That's all very well, but you're interfering with my trade.'
Bert Thomas, *London Opinion*, 9 January 1915

The Morgan Toad
Simplicissimus (Munich), 9 May 1916

Boer and Briton Too
General Botha (composing telegram to the Kaiser): 'Just off to repel another raid.
Your customary wire of congratulation should be addressed:
"British Headquarters – German South-West Africa."'
F.H.Townsend, *Punch*, 30 September 1914

**The Last of the German Boarhound; or the
South African Lion's Latest Shikar**
Hindi Punch, 1915

Meanwhile, after repelling raids into Allied-held South Africa from German
South-West Africa (now Namibia) in 1914, British Empire forces were faced with a
major rebellion by Boer (Dutch South African) extremists in their ranks, leading
to the desertion of 11,000 Allied troops to the German side in the autumn of that
year. However, after suppressing the rebellion, the Allied commander, General
Louis Botha, launched a major invasion of 21,000 South African troops into
German South-West Africa in March 1915. By 12 May they had occupied
Windhoek, the capital, and by the end of July the whole country had fallen to
the Allies.

The drawing by Townsend *(above)* alludes to the Kruger Telegram of the Boer
War when the Kaiser congratulated the Boer leader Paul Kruger on repelling the
British Jameson Raid. General Louis Botha was not only Prime Minister of the
Union of South Africa (then part of the British Empire) but was also in charge of
its army, the only serving premier worldwide to take this dual role. As a Boer he
had fought against the British – with German support – during the Boer War but
was now on the side of the Allies against the Germans.

The Indian cartoon *(above right)* has the British Lion defeating the German
Boarhound (*shikar* means 'hunt') while the German view *(right)* has John Bull
leading a calf marked 'Botha' to the slaughter. Shown opposite is a recruiting
poster printed in Pretoria.

The 'Grateful' Boer, Botha
(Old Proverb) 'Only the most foolish calves choose
their own slaughterer'
Kladderadatsch (Berlin), 1914

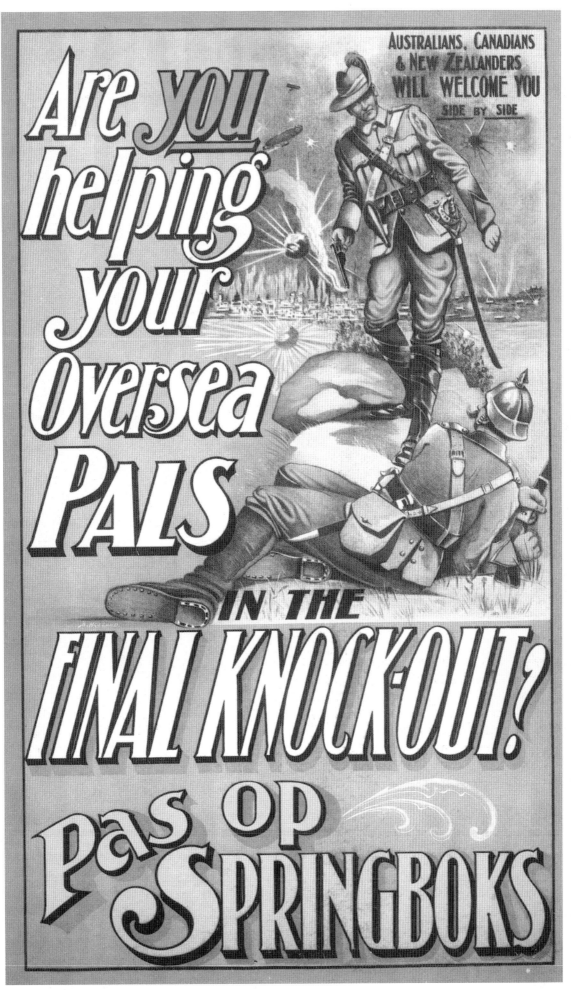

South African recruitment poster, 1915

There were many reports of breaches of the Hague Convention (precursor to the Geneva Convention) on the humane conduct of war during the conflict, especially of the treatment of prisoners by the Germans. The two British posters *(below)* by David Wilson (1873-1935) – who also drew for the *Daily Chronicle*, *Graphic* and *Passing Show* – emphasise this. (Wilson's Red Cross drawing is a very rare British example of a German woman being portrayed as unkind to those in need and is made doubly powerful by the fact that she is a nurse.) By contrast the German cartoon *(right)* – in which Kitchener addresses Prime Minister Herbert Asquith and First Sea Lord Winston Churchill – claims it is all British propaganda.

The Dutch cartoon by Raemaekers *(opposite)* comments on the very real execution by firing squad, on 12 October 1915, of the British nurse Edith Cavell. Resident in Brussels since 1907, Cavell remained in the city after war broke out and after the German occupation was arrested for helping more than 200 allied prisoners-of-war to escape to neutral Holland. Her death caused a storm of controversy and a statue was later erected in her honour outside the National Portrait Gallery in London. (Note that the pigs around her corpse not only wear *pickelhaube* helmets but the one in the foreground even has an Iron Cross pinned to its tail.)

Lord Kitchener Distorts the Evidence
'This man says that the Germans treat their wounded prisoners well. But you see, sir, that they have tortured him so terribly that he has lost his senses.'
German cartoon, c.1915

Once a German – Always a German!
David Wilson, British poster, 1917

Red Cross or Iron Cross?
David Wilson, British poster, 1915

Thrown to the Swine
The Martyred Nurse
Louis Raemaekers, 1915

Bent, But Not Broken
*(A German General says that the German line in the West
has been bent, but not broken)*
The German: 'Not broken; but, ach, Gott, I've got mein belly full!'
Melbourne Punch, 1915

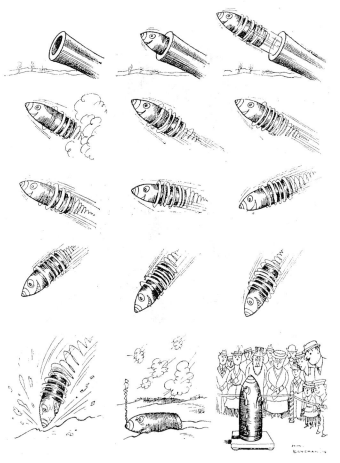

The Dud
H.M.Bateman, *Punch*, 12 June 1918

Almost Too Late
Mr Lloyd George Only Just Catches the Victoria Bus
F.H.Townsend, *Punch*, 29 December 1915

A Labour of Love
'Aren't you ashamed of yourself, Sammy, to sell such shells to your old
friend? Even the devil could not hit a German with them.'
'Well, what did you expect with three months' credit?'
Kladderadatsch (Berlin), n.d.

While the Second Battle of Ypres was still in progress the Allies launched the major Artois Offensive in May 1915 over a sector of the Western Front stretching from Arras to Lille in an attempt to break through the German lines. The French, under General Joffre, attacked between Arras and Lens while the British, under Haig, attacked at Neuve Chapelle towards the Aubers Ridge. However, shortages of shells in the British sector meant that the preliminary barrage lasted only 40 minutes and they were unable to exploit their initial success. Also at this time many shells were discovered to be faulty (duds) and did not explode due to poor workmanship in the munitions factories. There were 11,000 British casualties before the attack was called off.

An article in *The Times* on 14 May 1915 criticised the lack of high-explosive shells and blamed the BEF's initial failure in the Artois

Offensive on this. This so-called 'Shell Scandal' led to heated debate in Britain and Asquith's Liberal government fell, to be replaced by a new Coalition government on 25 May. Asquith remained as Prime Minister, but the new Cabinet now contained 12 Liberals and 8 Conservatives. Lloyd George was made Minister for Munitions.

In the Australian cartoon *(top left)*, the Kaiser gets a shell labelled 'Joffre's Attack' in his stomach while in the London *Punch (top right)* H.M.Bateman satirises the 'dud' situation. Townsend's cartoon *(above left)* has Lloyd George – holding a shell – only just managing to catch the Victory (Victoria) bus. The German cartoon*(above right)*, meanwhile, suggests that some dud shells were sold to Britain by the USA.

A Souvenir
German cartoon, 1915

'Oh God! It is not easy to be an English Minister of Marine all day.'
German cartoon, 1915

One of the casualties of the new government was Winston Churchill who was dismissed as First Lord of the Admiralty because of the Dardanelles failure. He subsequently joined the Army and in November 1915, Major Churchill of the Oxfordshire Yeomanry joined Sir John French's headquarters in France. He later served as a Battalion Commander in the 6th Royal Scots Fusiliers in Flanders from January to May 1916. French, who had commanded the BEF since it had landed in France in 1914 was himself criticised over the BEF's part in the Artois Offensive and was dismissed in December 1915 to be replaced by Sir Douglas Haig.

The two German cartoons *(above)* make fun of Churchill while Townsend *(right)* has him joining French's staff. (The French title means: 'Churchill goes off to war.')

Churchill S'en Va-t-en Guerre
Winston (through force of nautical habit, to Sir John French): 'Come aboard, sir!'
F.H.Townsend, *Punch*, 24 November 1915

81

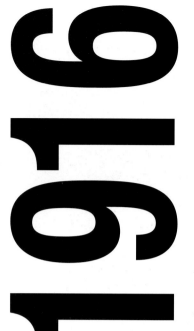

BY 1916 THE WAR of attrition on the Western Front seemed to have turned into an endless, remorseless, mincing machine. The Germans' main offensive to break the deadlock this year was an assault against the fortress city of Verdun in France led by troops under the command of the Kaiser's son, Crown Prince William. However, this turned into a long siege which resulted in great loss of life. To try and relieve the pressure on Verdun the British spearheaded 'the Big Push' – a massive offensive on the Somme – but this proved equally disastrous, with more than 400,000 British troops reported killed, wounded or missing. Such was the stalemate that the Germans began to build a huge defencework, known as the Hindenburg Line.

Meanwhile, on the Eastern Front, an attack by the Russian General Brusilov had considerable success against the Austro-Hungarian and German forces, taking 375,000 prisoners and 15,000 square miles of territory, and there were Italian gains at Gorizia. The beleaguered French and British were also cheered by the death of the aged Austro-Hungarian Emperor Franz Joseph, the entry of Romania, Greece and Portugal into the war on the Allied side, and the arrival of half a million troops from Canada. The replacement of General Joffre with General Nivelle as the head of Allied forces on the Western Front improved morale, as did the appointment of David Lloyd George as British Prime Minister in place of Asquith. However, the death of Lord Kitchener was a major blow and British confidence was further shaken by the Easter Uprising in Ireland.

Another more promising uprising for the Allied war effort was the Arab Revolt against Turkish rule which began this year and led to the capture of Mecca, and the taking of the important Turkish port of Aqaba by Hejaz Arabs, led by the charismatic British Colonel T.E.Lawrence ('Lawrence of Arabia').

On the home front a mass attack by 16 huge German airships resulted in one being brought down in flames by a British pilot in full view of thousands of Londoners, while at sea the British Home Fleet and the German High Seas Fleet met at the Battle of Jutland. Though the victory was not a decisive one, the German Fleet would not leave harbour again for the rest of the war.

German 'Freedom of the Seas'
Uncle Sam: 'That's their idea of a new Statue of Liberty, is it? Reckon it won't do on this side of the herring pond, anyway.'
David Wilson, *Passing Show*, 20 May 1916

Despite the outcry which had followed the sinking of the SS *Lusitania* in 1915, the German government continued to sanction the actions of its submarines, claiming that the British blockade was illegal and arguing that the 'Freedom of the Seas' was a universal right. However, Chancellor Bethmann-Hollweg argued against German Navy chief Von Tirpitz's wish to return to an unrestricted submarine warfare campaign as it was felt this would be likely to precipitate the involvement of the USA in the war. This led to the resignation of Von Tirpitz on 16 March. None the less, there were again international protests when neutral passenger ships – such as the Dutch liner *Tubantia* (sunk without warning off Harwich on 16 March) – were attacked.

The Dutch cartoon opposite shows Germania (complete with the Iron Cross given to submariners and wearing the Kaiser's crown) claiming that such reports are false (*'Es ist nicht wahr'* means 'It is not true') while grabbing the *Tubantia* to add to the other Dutch ships already at the bottom of the ocean. (In the drawing by David Wilson note the torch labelled *Kultur* and the book of *Laws of Frightfulness.*)

P. Vanderhem, *De Nieuwe Amsterdammer*, 25 March 1916

The French garrison city of Verdun on the River Meuse, 150 miles east of Paris, had huge walls and was surrounded by 19 forts. Believing, correctly, that the French would defend it at all costs (it had been the last fortress to fall in the Franco-Prussian War), the Germans decided to launch a protracted siege that would eventually 'bleed the French Army white'. Thus, in what was to prove the last major German offensive on the Western Front until 1918, massed German troops under the overall command of Crown Prince Wilhelm attacked on 21 February 1916. In what was then the biggest ever bombardment in wartime, a million German shells were fired on the first day. Despite this and the use of a new weapon – the flame-thrower – by the Germans, the French under General Henri-Philippe Pétain defended their positions stoically (Pétain is alleged to have declared '*Ils ne passeront pas*' – 'They shall not pass'). It is estimated that three-quarters of the entire French Army served at Verdun at some point in the battle (they were sent in on rotation) and in 10 months of the siege (until 18 December) around 900,000 soldiers were killed or wounded (550,000 French, 434,000 German).

Pétain came to prominence again later as the leader of Vichy France in World War II. Other famous people involved at Verdun were the 25-year-old Charles de Gaulle (wounded and captured by the Germans) and a young Friedrich von Paulus (later Field Marshal and attacker of Stalingrad in World War II).

One of the confectionery specialities made in the town of Verdun is a hard sweet known as a *dragée*, or sugar-coated almond. The artist 'Lig' *(opposite, top left)* has drawn Crown Prince Wilhelm as a monkey wearing the hat of the Death's Head Hussars (his own regiment) but unable to crack open the sweet labelled 'Verdun' (note the Iron Cross pinned to his tail). Sullivan *(opposite, right)* has adapted the famous address given to the emperors of Ancient Rome by gladiators when entering the arena ('Hail, Caesar, we who are about to die salute you'). In this version it is the already dead troops that salute him as they parade past the Kaiser and a huge siege gun. The German cartoon *(above)* takes a different stance as a German soldier hacks the branch that is holding the French officer.

French War Dispatch
'The situation gives no cause for uneasiness'
Simplicissimus (Munich), 1916

His Secret Sorrow
'I reckon this bloke must 'ave caught 'is face against
some of them forts at Verdun!'
Bruce Bairnsfather, *Bystander*, 1916

**'They are tough these
"Dragées of Verdun"!'**
Lig (Lignières), *Le Journal*, (Paris) 1916

'Ave, Kaiser, Imperatore Moriture, Mortui Te Salutamus'
Edmund J.Sullivan, *The Kaiser's Garland* (1915)

A Game of Patience
Frank Holland, *John Bull*, c.1916

Still Captive at Kiel
Bert Thomas, *London Opinion*, 17 June 1916

The Battle of Jutland (or Skagerrak as the Germans called it) was Britain's first great fleet action since the Battle of Trafalgar a century earlier and such was its strategic importance that it was said that the British commander, Admiral Jellicoe, was the only man who could lose the war in an afternoon. If he failed, the German Navy would have total command of the sea. This would mean that the blockade against Germany would be lifted, British troops in Europe would be cut off from their supply lines and Britain itself could be invaded.

The battle began on 31 May 1916 when, in an attempt to get the British Grand Fleet to leave its safe anchorage at Scapa Flow in the Orkneys (where it cut off all German exits from the North Sea and hence routes to Germany's colonies worldwide), Admiral Scheer, newly appointed Commander-in-Chief of the German High Seas Fleet, led his ships out of their Baltic base on the Kiel Canal bound for Jutland, off the Danish coast.

However, unknown to the Germans, the British had acquired a German Navy code book from the light cruiser *Magdeburg*

(captured in 1914 by the Russians after it ran aground in fog on the island of Odenseholm in the Gulf of Finland) and could track their every move. The battle involved 250 warships, 25 admirals and 100,000 men. The Royal Navy lost 14 ships (112,000 tons) and nearly 7000 men while the Germans lost 11 ships (62,000 tons) and nearly 3000 men. However, though technically the German Navy won the encounter in terms of tonnage sunk and lives lost, the German fleet was thus effectively from that time penned in by the Royal Navy.

Frank Holland (fl.1895-1933) was the main political cartoonist on the highly patriotic *John Bull* magazine which was edited by Horatio Bottomley. *John Bull* reached its largest circulation ever during the Great War and Bottomley himself was a superb orator, especially for Army recruitment. However, he was imprisoned in 1922 for fraud connected with wartime Victory Bonds. In Holland's cartoon *(above left)*, the German boy has left his clothes on land marked 'German Colonies' and is unable to retrieve them. A similar message is given in Thomas's drawing *(above right)*.

Not surprisingly, the German press took a different view of the conflict. Both German cartoons on this page show the defeat of John Bull (note the Union Jack loincloth in the drawing from *Simplicissimus*).

Return from Skagerrak
Simplicissimus (Munich), 20 July 1916

A Pill for Bill
British postcard, c.1916

Sent Home, 31 May 1916
A.Roeseler, *Fliegende Blätter*, 30 June 1916

Unappetising
Moments when the Savoy, the Alhambra, and the Piccadilly Grill
seem very far away (the offensive starts in half an hour)
Bruce Bairnsfather, *Bystander*, 1916

The First Battle of the Somme – 'the Big Push'- was the first test of Lord Kitchener's New Army which had been sent in to replace the BEF which by 1916 had largely been destroyed. Designed to take the pressure off the French at Verdun, it was a British-led offensive of British Empire (including Canadian, Australian and New Zealand) and French troops under Sir Douglas Haig over a 30-mile front from Amiens to Peronne. It began on 23 June 1916 with a massive artillery barrage (nearly two million shells) which was so loud that windows rattled in London 160 miles away. (However it was later discovered that 30% of the British-made shells were in fact duds.) Casualties were enormous. On the first day alone there were 57,000 British casualties (of which 19,000 were killed), the biggest ever loss in a single day by the British Army. The battle lasted just over four months (140 days), until 13 November, and the total number of Allied casualties were 415,000 British and 195,000 French.

Amongst those firing at each other on the Somme were Henry Williamson (who later wrote *Tarka the Otter*), future Prime Minister Harold Macmillan (who was wounded), Robert Graves (who was left for dead) and Adolf Hitler (who was also wounded). Those killed during the battle included Asquith's son Lieutenant Raymond Asquith (19 September 1916) and the short-story writer Saki (H.H.Munro) whose last words were 'Put out that bloody cigarette!' Siegfried Sassoon won a Military Cross on the Somme and Lt-Col Bernard Freyberg (a high-ranking general in World War II) won a VC.

Despite the huge losses, the Somme was seen as a limited Allied success and the new recruits acquitted themselves well. However, Kitchener would not live to see the future glories of his New Army as he was himself killed on 5 June 1916. Ironically he died not on the battlefield but was drowned at sea off the Orkney Islands when his ship struck a mine.

'Dai Pepper on the Somme'
J.M.Staniforth in Captain T.E.Elias (ed.)
New Year Souvenir of the Welsh Division (1917)

Welshman J.M.Staniforth (1863-1921) was the political cartoonist on the *Western Mail* (published in Cardiff) from 1893 until his death. As well as drawing political cartoons, he also created the football-playing character Dai Pepper for the paper's Saturday football supplement, *Football Express*. In Captain T.E.Elias' *New Year Souvenir of the Welsh Division* (1917) – a special souvenir volume published by the *Western Mail* for the Welsh Division of the British Army – Dai Pepper (note the Welsh leek in his hat) is seen single-handedly capturing a group of German soldiers from a dugout during the Battle of the Somme while a British bulldog proudly carries a German helmet in its mouth. Meanwhile, Bairnsfather and Townsend have drawn two almost identical cartoons *(below)* to celebrate the victorious 'New Army' Tommy – even down to the German helmet on his bayonet and a bandage around his left arm.

Bruce Bairnsfather (cover) in Captain A.J.Dawson,
Somme Battle Stories (1916)

Well Done, the New Army!
F.H.Townsend, *Punch*, 12 July 1916

'I'll Go Too!'
Irish recruiting poster, c.1916

John Bull, the Good Shepherd
'Oh shepherd, dear shepherd, on our dead bones
Thou soundest lustily such dread tones!'
Richard Rost, *Jugend*, 27 October 1916

The Easter Uprising of Irish nationalists in Dublin could not have come at a worse time for the Allied war effort. The question of Irish independence had been discussed heatedly for many years and in July 1914 Erskine Childers (author of the 1903 novel *The Riddle of the Sands* about a German invasion of Britain) had succeeded in illegally shipping 900 rifles from Germany to Ireland.

In August 1914 the Irish nationalist and former British consul, Sir Roger Casement, wrote to the Kaiser offering to join the German cause and raise an Irish legion against the British in return for Irish independence. After meetings in Berlin and the USA he had suggested – with financial support from Irish Americans – a landing in Ireland by 25,000 German troops with 50,000 guns. In the event the Germans decided only to send 20,000 guns but these were caught by a British patrol boat. However, despite only limited arms an uprising went ahead in Dublin. On 24 April 1916 fighting broke out and the Dublin Post Office was taken. Martial law was introduced on 27 April and the rebellion was crushed by 1 May (both Casement and Childers were later tried for treason and executed). During the Great War 200,000 Irish – both Catholic and Protestant – fought for Britain (30,000 were killed).

The Dutch cartoon opposite – 'John Bull's Foot' – has John Bull nursing a gouty left foot marked 'Ireland' as soldiers march off to battle behind (the implication being that he would also like to join the big spring offensive (hence the rifle) but that the situation in Ireland tied up British troops. (Note the Johnny [*sic*] Walker whisky bottle.) Meanwhile, the German cartoon *(above right)*, has John Bull dressed as a Scottish piper with Ireland the latest head added to his deadly bagpipes after India, France and Egypt.

In the Irish recruiting poster *(above left)*, an Irish gentleman, wearing riding boots and carrying a crop, offers to enlist in the British Army (note the shamrocks and historic tower, a feature of Irish churches).

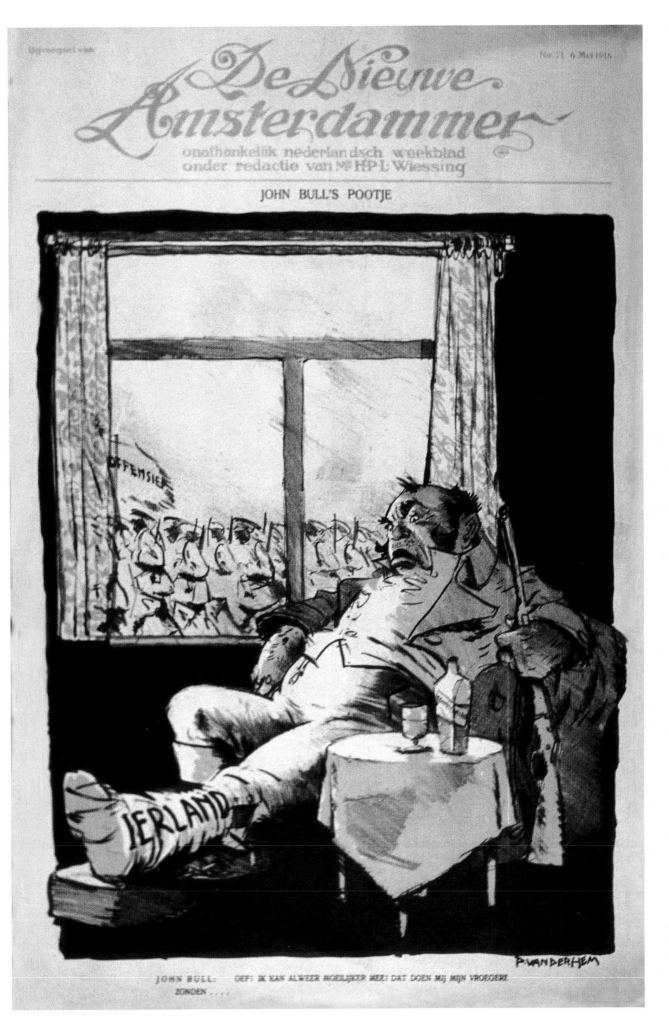

John Bull's Foot
John Bull: 'Ouch! I always have trouble with this foot! It's a legacy of my earlier life...'
P. Vanderhem, *De Nieuwe Amsterdammer*, 6 May 1916

Ex-Gardener (concluding letter to his late employer):
'Well, Madam. I don't think I have much more to tell you, except that there's good soil out here for roses – just the thing for them. I said as soon as I saw it, "that's the soil for roses".'
F.H.Townsend, *Punch*, 20 December 1916

Trench Philosophy
'Bill, what's the difference between an optimist and a pessimist?'
'Well, it's this way, 'Arry. When the Bosches are strafing, a hoptimist thinks the shells are just being fired indiscriminate-like at no one in partic'lar, while a pessimist 'e thinks every shell is meant for 'isself.'
F.H.Townsend, *Punch*, 20 September 1916

Anxiety
'If only they can hold out!'
'Who?'
'The civilians.'
Jean-Louis Forain, 9 January 1915

By 1916 a certain mood of cynicism had entered the troops on both sides of the conflict on the Western Front, as the cartoons on these pages from Britain, Holland, France and Germany show. In the German trench drawing an old soldier hoists a turnip wearing a German helmet to draw fire.

A Letter From the German Trenches
'We have gained a good bit; our cemeteries now extend as far as the sea.'
Louis Raemaekers, c.1916

Im Schützengraben.
Eine gute Anlage.

In the Dugout
German cartoon, 1916

German cartoon, c.1916

'Father, is it still a long way to the Beresina?
Louis Raemaekers, 1916

München, 29. August 1916   Preis 35 Pfg.   21. Jahrgang Nr. 22

SIMPLICISSIMUS

Begründet von Albert Langen und Th. Th. Heine

Englisches Spielzeug

English Toys
'Look, Mr Bull, the Russian Bear is losing wind again!'
Wilhelm Schutz, *Simplicissimus* (Munich), 20 August 1916

The Bear: **'Glad to see you out again. I feel better myself!'**
Robert Carter, *New York Evening Sun*, 18 January 1916

Though the war had reached stalemate on the Western Front there was still considerable activity elsewhere. To relieve the pressure on the French at Verdun, the Russian High Command launched two major offensives on the Eastern Front. The first, beginning with an eight-hour bombardment by 1200 guns and followed by an attack using 350,000 troops, took place in the spring around Lake Naroch but the results were only limited. Far more successful was the summertime Brusilov Offensive (the only successful offensive of the war to be named after a real person). Led by General Aleksey Brusilov, the Russian Army entered Galicia on 4 June 1916 and by August had captured 375,000 German and Austro-Hungarian prisoners and had taken 15,000 square miles of territory.

The drawing *(bottom left)* by Robert Carter (1875-1918), who died during the war at the age of 44, expresses the increasing mood of confidence by the Russians, while Raemaekers *(above left)* portrays the desperate situation of the Kaiser and Crown Prince Wilhelm. (Napoleon had crossed the River Beresina into Russia with half a million men in 1812 – when he recrossed it on the retreat from Moscow he had very few left.) The German cartoon *(above right)* – featuring John Bull and President Wilson with an inflatable French cockerel and Russian bear – takes a different view of the war on the Eastern Front.

Encouraged by the success of the Russian Brusilov Offensive, Romania joined the Allies and declared war against Austria-Hungary on 27 August 1916. Though the Prussian-born King Ferdinand of Romania had strong Austro-German connections, his wife Marie was British (a cousin of George V) and had considerable political influence. The Bank of England had made a loan of £5 million to Romania in 1915 and Marie negotiated Romania's entry into the war on the Allied side in return for various territorial claims from Hungary.

At first the Romanian Army met with some success as 400,000 troops marched into Transylvania, but after Bulgaria declared war on Romania in September a combined force of Bulgarian, Turkish, Austro-Hungarian and German forces mounted a series of counterattacks. By 6 December Bucharest had fallen and most of Romania was occupied by the Central Powers who not only took control of its natural sources (including oil), but also stripped the population of all food and raw materials. In consequence, by late 1918 more than 500,000 civilians had died of starvation and other causes under the occupation.

In the drawing for the neutral Dutch weekly *De Nieuwe Amsterdammer (right)*, German Chancellor Bethmann-Hollweg is seen chained up in stocks while death and destruction rage around him in Romania. Around his neck hangs a torn-up agreement on official German Reich paper that says 'Guarantee [of Neutrality] for Belgium', signed by Wilhelm, King of Prussia. (Bethmann-Hollweg had voiced his concern about the brutal occupation of Romania which began to show marked similarities to the occupation of Belgium.) Meanwhile, Townsend *(below left)* portrays Germany as a greedy young man holding a knobkerry as a thin girl representing Austria looks on. (At this stage in the war the Royal Navy blockade meant that very little food or other supplies were reaching Germany and Austria.)

Virtuous Ecstasy Towards Romania
Bethmann joins with Romania to complain about 'political circumstances in which the words of ministers and kings are not worth anything'.
De Nieuwe Amsterdammer, 7 October 1916

The Apple of Discord
Austria: 'Where did you get that?'
Germany: 'Spoils of Romania.'
Austria: 'Well, if it's not big enough to split you might let us have the core.'
Germany: 'There ain't going to be no core.'
F.H.Townsend, *Punch*, 24 January 1917

David and Goliath
The Romanian Hedgehog Gets His Back Up
Frank Holland, *Reynolds News*, 1916

Italy's Day!
F.H.Townsend, *Punch*, 16 August 1916

The Order of the Boot
Esquella de la Torratxa (Barcelona), 1916

Reciprocity
Death: 'Thank you, friends, for what you have done for me.
I will now do as much for you.'
Desiderio, *Il 420* (Florence), 1916

**Franz Joseph Departs to the Front to Cheer His
Troops. But Will He Get There?**
Loukomorye (Petrograd), 1916

After a number of defeats the Italians achieved their best results so far in the war at
the 6th Battle of the Isonzo (also called the Battle of Gorizia) in August 1916, taking
Gorizia and a considerable amount of territory from the Austro-Hungarians but with
losses of about 50,000 on each side. By this time the Austro-Hungarian Emperor
(now 86) was in extremely fragile health. He died on 21 November 1916 and was
succeeded by his great-nephew Karl. On 28 August Italy also declared war on Germany.

Meanwhile, at the end of 1915 the defeated Serbian Army of 200,000 men had begun to retreat south-westwards through the mountains in a bid to reach Albania. Thousands died of cold and starvation before they reached their goal in early January, from where they were evacuated by French ships to the Greek island of Corfu (which had been occupied by French forces despite neutral Greece's protests) and then on to Salonika where they joined Allied troops. From here, in September they formed part of an Allied force that launched a counterattack against Bulgarian and German troops in Macedonia, and Serbian and French troops recaptured the city of Monastir in November.

One of Those Balkan Muddles

His father was a Czech, but his mother was a Serb. He used to live in Bohemia, but his sympathies are all Italian. Fought for the Austrians in Galicia owing to his love of the Croats and Magyars. Suspected of being a Slovak or Ruthenian, he was sent to the Italian front, where he slipped on a banana skin in Gorizia and was captured.
Bruce Bairnsfather, *Bystander*, 1916

Ferdinand's Fright
'Help! Help! I thought he was a corpse!'
Owen Aves, *Passing Show*, 1916

**The Bulldog Establishes His Ascendancy
Both Aerial and Moral**
Jack Walker, *The Daily Graphic Special War Cartoons, No. 6* (1915)

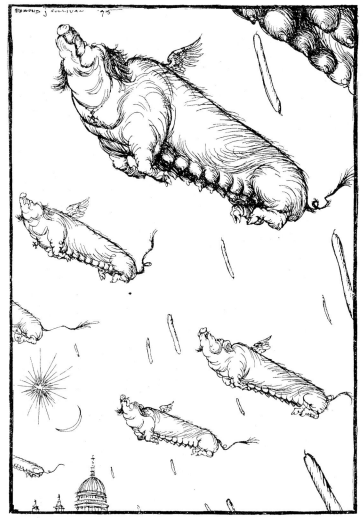

'When the Pigs Begin to Fly'
Die Blutwurst
Edmund J.Sullivan, *The Kaiser's Garland* (1915)

The Zeppelin Rain on Ipswich
Missed Another Baby
W.A.Rogers, *New York Herald*, 1 May 1915

Aircraft of many kinds had been in use by both the Allied forces and the Central Powers almost from the beginning of the war. These included man-carrying aeroplanes, kites, kite balloons and non-rigid self-propelled balloons for artillery-spotting, anti-submarine, anti-mine and coastal patrol duties. However, the most significant attacking force in the opening years of the conflict were the enormous dirigibles (rigid balloons built around a frame) created by Count Ferdinand von Zeppelin (1838-1917) and named after him. Zeppelin had made his first ascent in a balloon in the USA while he was serving in the Union Army as a balloon observer during the American Civil War and it was here that he had got the idea for creating a series of balloons held together with a frame which could be steered.

The first raids over Britain by Zeppelin airships took place in December 1914 and in January 1915 the Kaiser gave permission for them to attack London and other British targets. The first raid on London was on 26 May 1915 when a single airship dropped a ton of bombs, killing 7 and injuring 35. Over the next year or so there were increasing attacks by as many as 11 airships at a time. Less than a decade earlier, science-fiction writers such as H.G.Wells had imagined this kind of attack. (Zeppelin was not the only manufacturer of airships though most were called Zeppelins anyway. Others included Schütte-Lanz and Parseval.)

One of the most spectacular occasions involving a Zeppelin occurred on the night of 3 September 1916 when 500 bombs were dropped between Gravesend near London and Peterborough in Lincolnshire. However, what made this evening remarkable was that one of the airships – a huge Schütte-Lanz SL11 (nearly 600 feet long and 80 feet high) – was shot down near London by a British aeroplane piloted by William Leefe Robinson and its destruction was witnessed by thousands of civilians below (Robinson won a VC for this act, the only one ever awarded for an act on British soil).

Many similar successes followed and this, together with improved air defences and explosive shells which set fire to the highly inflammable hydrogen gas used to fill the airships' balloons, led to the gradual decline in Zeppelin attacks – especially after the death of Peter Strasser, head of the Zeppelin fleet, who died over London in March 1917. By 1918 there were only four airship raids on Britain, the last being on the night of 5 August.

In Sullivan's drawing *(opposite, top left)* the airships are seen as female pigs dropping bombs in the shape of blood sausages (*Blutwurst*, known as 'black pudding' in Britain, is made from pigs' blood) at night (note the crescent moon) over St Paul's Cathedral. In Jack Walker's drawing *(opposite, top right)* the German dachshund airship carries 'Bombs for British Babies' while the British bulldog aeroplane has 'Bombs for Places of Military Significance'. The American cartoon *(opposite, bottom)* by W.A.Rogers (1854-1931) also takes this stance, while the Russian poster *(right)* shows Allied aircraft attacking a Zeppelin at night.

The Air War
Russian poster, c.1915

The lady in the striped dress, referring to an officer in our 'Amazon Corps' who has just passed:
'That's our Adjutant, Mrs Robinson. I suppose she didn't recognise me in mufti.'
Claude Shepperson, *Punch*, 12 July 1916

The Great War changed the position of women in society for ever. Before it the Suffragette Movement had campaigned for many years for equal rights for women, especially the right to vote (suffrage). With so many of Britain's men at the front, their jobs at home – working as public-transport drivers, in munitions factories, on farms, and in many other roles – were taken over by women who quickly showed that they were perfectly capable of doing the tasks they were given. In March 1915 the British government issued an appeal for women to join a register of Women for War Service and by August 1916 more than 750,000 women worked at jobs formerly held by men. Demonstrations by women for the Right to Serve also led to the setting-up of women's non-combatant armed forces. The first ever British women's battalions – nicknamed 'the Amazon Corps' – were formed in 1917. By the end of the war British women served in the First Aid Nursing Yeomanry (FANY), the Volunteer Aid Detachment (VAD), the Women's Land Army, Queen Mary's Army Auxiliary Corps, the Women's Royal Naval Service (WRNS) and the Women's Royal Air Force (WRAF). In Russia women also served in actual combat roles, notably in the Women's Battalion of the Russian Army led by Maria Botchkareva. Both British and German cartoonists were quick to mock the idea of women in uniform.

Second-Lieut. Mabel Smells Powder (No Novelty)
'There you are, Bert; I told you we'd 'ave 'em 'ere before we'd finished.'
Bruce Bairnsfather, *Bystander*, 1916

The Girl Behind the Man Behind the Gun
British poster, n.d.

English Women's Troops
'We are lost, dear ladies – there is a mouse!'
B.Gestwicki, *Lustige Blätter*, 1915

The Women's Regiment
Lustige Blätter, 1915

The Great Offensive
Simplicissimus (Munich), 25 July 1916

Once the Lion was King of the Desert
Simplicissimus (Munich), 16 May 1916

Oil is very important for mechanised warfare, so as soon as Turkey declared war Britain attacked Turkish-held Mesopotamia (Iraq) – a major oil-producing country – in an attempt to capture its oil supplies. At first the force, comprising Indian and British troops, had considerable success and took Basra before heading for the capital, Baghdad, some 500 miles away. However, with temperatures soaring to 120°F they decided to fall back to Kut-el-Amara on the River Tigris to wait for reinforcements, reaching the city on 3 December 1915. Unfortunately, the reinforcements did not arrive in time and on 29 April 1916 the Allied garrison of 13,000 men under General Sir Charles Townshend surrendered because of lack of food and supplies.

As can be seen from these two cartoons from *Simplicissimus*, the Germans made much of the catastrophic defeat of the Allied force, which had a similar impact on morale to that of the Allied defeat at Tobruk in

North Africa in World War II. (Baghdad was finally captured by the Allies on 11 March 1917.)

This year also saw the beginning of the Arab Revolt which had been inspired by the British promise of independence to Hejaz Arabs if they threw off Turkish rule. British-led forces soon captured the holy city of Mecca but the Turkish garrison at Medina held out. The British Colonel T.E.Lawrence (Lawrence of Arabia) led railway sabotages by the Arab tribesmen against the Turks and, after a seven-week journey across 600 miles of the Hejaz Desert at the height of the summer, took the important Turkish port of Aqaba (whose guns only pointed to the sea). This success led to the Arab forces being invited to join the Allied assault on Jerusalem.

To break the blockade of Germany by the Royal Navy, which prevented supplies of raw material and food reaching the country by sea, a huge (200-foot-long) unarmed submarine, the *Deutschland* – which could carry 1000 tons of cargo – was sent from Kiel in Germany to Baltimore in the USA (then neutral) in the summer of 1916. As it was the first submarine ever to cross the Atlantic, when it docked in Baltimore on 9 July its crew were treated like visiting celebrities. For three weeks dinners and parties were given in their honour and Captain Koenig was even invited to meet the President. After taking on supplies the submarine returned to Germany in August and managed to evade capture by the Allies.

In Beuttler's cartoon *(right)* part of the cargo of the *Deutschland* is seen to be the fleeing Kaiser himself, while the German drawing *(below right)* has the *Deutschland* slipping between John Bull's legs.

The True Story of the *Deutschland*
I. Loading II. The US Customs Officer makes a little discovery
E.G.O.Beuttler, *The Merry Mariners* (1917)

The New Line Bremen-Baltimore
'Hurrah! *Deutschland!*'
Julius Diez, *Jugend*, 15 July 1916

Nothing Doing

John Bull: 'No, William, that little dodge won't work. When you want peace,
you can have it – on our terms. Meanwhile, let's get on with the fighting.'

Frank Holland, 1916

The Enfant Terrible

Kladderadatsch (Berlin), 1917

The German Offer

'Kamerad! Kamerad!'

Le Rire (Paris), 1917

'Personally I am so keen for peace that I would even be willing
to accept the status quo of 1914.'
'That's fine by me – but in that case can I have my leg back!'
La Baïonnette, 1916

A JAPANESE VIEW OF PEACE

Germany: 'Look here! It's the year-end bargain.
The asking price may be a bit fancy, but it won't hurt
you to look at it, will it?'
Jiji (Tokyo), 23 January 1917

In a speech to the Reichstag on 12 December 1916 the German Chancellor Theobald von Bethmann-Hollweg, on behalf of the Central Powers, called for peace talks on the ground that continued fighting was futile. However, the conditions attached to these suggestions were unsatisfactory to the Allies and were rejected. Then, on 18 December President Wilson, on behalf of the neutral USA, sent his own Peace Note to all the belligerent nations requesting a clear statement of their war aims as a preliminary to any ceasefire discussions. However, this only revealed how far apart the thinking was between the two sides and convinced the Germans that the only way forward was a return to unrestricted submarine warfare which they believed could win the war for them in six months.

These cartoons show various views of the peace offer as seen by British, French, Japanese, Austrian and German artists. The drawing from *Kladderadatsch (opposite, top right)* has French premier Aristide Briand as the fairy on the Christmas tree, supporting the German peace-feelers, while President Poincaré and French Army chief, Ferdinand Foch frown on the proposals.

Wilson and the Peace Angel
'Don't blame me, my beautiful child, Or greet me under the Palms!'
Die Muskete (Vienna), 1917

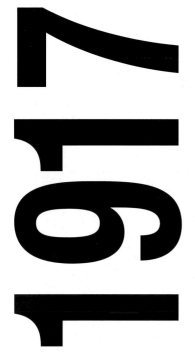

THE YEAR 1917 was one of great political changes in Europe, two of the most significant being the Russian Revolution in March – which led to the abdication of Tsar Nicholas II and the signing of an armistice between Russia and the Central Powers (thereby releasing thousands of troops to fight against the Allies elsewhere) – and the decision by President Wilson to bring the USA into the conflict on the side of the Allies in April. Other changes were the appointment of Georges Clemenceau ('The Tiger') as French Prime Minister and the resignation of Germany's long-serving Chancellor Theobald von Bethmann-Hollweg.

On the Western Front, trench warfare continued with limited success by the Allies after British-led attacks at the Battle of Arras in France and the Third Battle of Ypres (also known as Passchendaele) in Belgium – aimed at capturing the ports of Ostend and Zeebrugge. However, France's only major attack on the Western Front this year – the Nivelle Offensive in April, intended to take the wooded ridges known as the Chemin des Dames near Rheims – led to great loss of life and resulted in a mutiny involving half the entire French Army.

Meanwhile, on the Eastern Front, the Russian Kerensky Offensive in July failed (largely as a result of political unrest) and they were beaten again by a German counteroffensive (using new 'stormtroopers') which captured the important Baltic port of Riga in September. The Italians were also badly defeated at Caporetto, and the Allies' position was weakened still further when Romania signed an armistice with the Central Powers in December. Added to which, inferior aircraft led to great losses of Allied pilots to the newly formed German 'flying circus' fighter squadrons on the Western Front and huge Gotha long-range bombers began attacking England for the first time. To make matters worse the German government announced in February that it would once again launch a campaign of unrestricted submarine warfare in an attempt to starve Britain into surrender.

However the Central Powers did not have it all their own way in 1917. The massive German defencework known as the Hindenburg Line was broken by the first large-scale use of tanks by the British at Cambrai in Picardy, Turkish-held Baghdad and Jerusalem surrendered to the British, and Greece, Cuba, Brazil, Panama and China entered the war on the side of the Allies. In addition, new anti-submarine measures meant that the U-boat menace was finally beginning to be controlled.

Contradictory Talk
1. 'The U-boat war? Ha, ha! We have plenty of ships'
2. 'Give me your ships at once; otherwise I am lost'
Kladderadatsch (Berlin), 1917

After much heated discussion in the Reichstag, on 31 January 1917 Germany finally decided once again to launch an unrestricted submarine warfare campaign in an attempt to starve Britain into surrender. Knowing that this would undoubtedly lead to the USA's involvement in the war, Germany none the less gambled on the fact that it would be at least a year before US forces would be ready for combat, while an intensive submarine campaign could knock Britain out of the conflict within six months.

The decision staggered the civilised world as it was in defiance of all the traditional rules of war and against the Hague Convention on the conduct of warfare which Germany had signed. The initial impact on the Allies was huge – by April 1917 one ship in every four leaving UK ports failed to return, with 30,000 tons of shipping being sunk every day. Between May and December German U-boats sunk 500 British merchant ships and the country's reserves of wheat fell to six weeks' supply. However, by the end of the year the effectiveness of the U-boat menace was being severely compromised by the development by the Allies of new anti-submarine measures. These included convoys, amphibious spotter aircraft, depth-charges, hydrophones, Asdic underwater location devices, Q-ships (armoured ships disguised as merchantmen which opened fire on submarines with hidden cannon when they surfaced) and other new inventions.

The cartoonist Edward Beuttler goes one further and envisages *(top right)* a giant robot lobster-like marine tank in service with the undersea, or silent, service of the Royal Navy. Meanwhile, the German cartoon from *Lustige Blätter (below right)* has Americans queuing up in New York harbour to board the already overcrowded 'Theatre Ship' which promises the ultimate experience for pleasure-seekers. The sign reads 'Pleasure-trip to the prohibited area! Great sensation! U-boat attack guaranteed!' (Note that the passengers wear life-jackets over their theatre clothes.) The other two German cartoons comment on the success of the U-boat campaign. The drawing from *Jugend (below left)* alludes to the scene in Shakespeare's *Richard III* in which King Richard, unmounted and beaten at the battle of Bosworth Field cries out 'A horse, a horse, my kingdom for a horse!', while 'Contradictory Talk' *(opposite)* has John Bull stealing ships from Holland.

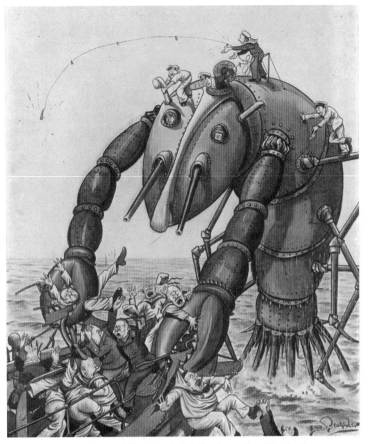

The 'Silent' Service's Little Surprise Packet
E.G.O.Beuttler, *The Merry Mariners* (1917)

The Last Act
Lloyd George: 'A ship! A ship! My kingdom for a ship!'
Jugend, 1917

The Theatre Ship
The Latest Thing for 'Pleasure-Seeking' Americans
J.Bahr, *Lustige Blätter*, 1917

The Pinch of War
Lady of the House (War Profiteer's wife, forlornly): 'They've just taken our third footman; and if any more of our men have to go we shall close the house and live at the Ritz until the War is over – *(brightly)* – However, we must all sacrifice something.'
Claude Shepperson, *Punch*, 10 January 1917

Reduced Import of Paper: What We May Come To
Mr Runciman: 'Ah well, one misses the old wealth of flattery; still one must make sacrifices for one's country!'
F.H.Townsend, *Punch*, 2 February 1916

Imitative Evolution on the Munition Worker's Allotment
Alfred Leete, *Punch*, 4 September 1918

British poster, 1917

With blockades at many ports and increasing attacks by German submarines on merchant shipping, stocks of some materials – such as paper and food (especially eggs, bread and potatoes) – began to become scarce in Britain. During 1916 more than 60% of Britain's food had been imported and in November that year a coarse 'war bread' had been introduced because of wheat shortages. In December 1916 a Ministry of Food had been set up and the public were encouraged to grow their own fruit and vegetables (many new allotment gardens were created for this purpose). However, though 'meatless days' were observed and a National Egg Day was introduced, there was no full-scale rationing in Britain until March 1918 (and for those who could afford it many scarce items could still be bought from war profiteers on the black market).

By contrast, rationing had been long-established in Germany and Austria-Hungary and *Ersatz* (substitute) food and goods were commonplace by 1917. These included roasted acorns (in place of coffee), limeflower tea and wooden-soled shoes. In fact, so scarce were some basic foodstuffs in Germany that the winter of 1916/17 was known as the 'Turnip Winter'.

In the multi-panelled German cartoon opposite the artist lampoons the British Royal Family's involvement in the Government food campaign (King George and Queen Mary planted potatoes on their Sandringham estate). The captions read as follows: 'The potato is washed...and sprayed with scent. Flunkies bring the Queen's potato and trowel. The Queen breaks the sod... and plants the potato. The Court manicurist removes all traces of the work.'

Meanwhile, commenting on paper shortages, Townsend *(above right)* imagines *The Times* (then a broadsheet newspaper) being reduced to the size of a pocket magazine. (The Liberal MP Walter Runciman – later 1st Viscount Runciman – was then President of the Board of Trade.) In Germany the real situation was far worse – by 13 February 1916 an estimated 2000 periodicals had ceased because of lack of paper.

Königin Mary von England baut Kartoffeln

Die Kartoffel wird gereinigt

und mit Wohlgerüchen besprengt.

Edelknaben überreichen der Königin Kartoffel und Handspaten.

Die Königin bearbeitet den Acker.

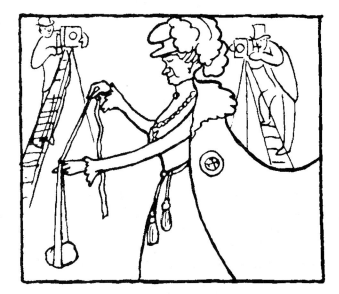

Einlegen der Kartoffel.

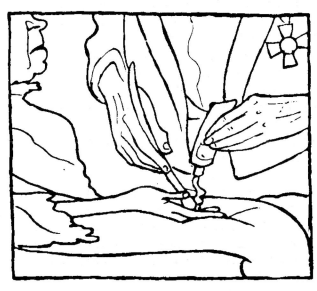

Der Hofmanicure entfernt die Arbeitsschwielen.

Queen Mary Plants a Potato
German cartoon, 1916

To France!
W.A.Rogers, *New York Herald*, 1917

The Trumpet That Shall Never call Retreat
Robert Carter, *Philadelphia Press*, 1917

**The United States of Great Britain
and America**
John Bull (to President Wilson): 'Bravo, sir! Delighted
to have you on our side.'
F.H.Townsend, *Punch*, 11 April 1917

Making Rapid Strides
Uncle Sam: 'Hold the fort, for I am coming!'
Frank Holland, *John Bull*, 11 August 1917

After three years of war the USA eventually abandoned its isolationism and joined in the conflict on the side of the Allies. Having cut diplomatic ties with Germany in February, soon after it had announced the recommencement of its unrestricted submarine warfare campaign, the USA declared war on 6 April 1917. However, the USA did not become a full ally of the British, French and Russians but preferred to be known as an 'Associate Power'.

As well as the German submarine campaign (five US ships had been sunk by U-boats in March 1917 alone), another important factor in the USA's decision to go to war was the furore caused by the publication in the US press of the so-called 'Zimmermann Letter' . This was a secret telegram sent by German Foreign Minister Arthur Zimmermann to the German Embassy in Mexico which had been intercepted and decoded by the British and passed on to the American government. In it Zimmermann instructed the ambassador to approach the Mexican Government and give assurances that, if Mexico declared war on the USA (with German support), the formerly Mexican territories of Texas, Arizona and New Mexico would be returned to it.

In Townsend's *Punch* cartoon *(opposite, bottom left)*, John Bull (with a Stars and Stripes flag in his lapel), welcomes President Wilson of the USA, armed to the teeth and carrying a bedroll. The words spoken by Uncle Sam in Frank Holland's drawing *(opposite, bottom right)* were originally credited to General W.T. Sherman, a Union commander during the American Civil War. Meanwhile, the German cartoon *(bottom right)* comments on the fact that though US General John Pershing (shown sitting in a waiting-room) had landed in France in June 1917 it would be many months before American troops arrived in force. ('Teddy' is former US President Theodore Roosevelt who in April 1917 offered to lead a corps of 25,000 US volunteers into immediate action on the Western Front.)

The US recruiting poster *(top right)* has a slavering giant German militarist gorilla (note the helmet and Kaiser-like moustache) carrying off a scantily dressed maiden and holding a club marked 'culture' while in the background can be seen a war-torn landscape and a ruined church. Though this image is very reminiscent of posters for the classic film *King Kong* (with Fay Wray in the arms of the monster ape) it was in fact produced 15 years before the movie.

Destroy This Mad Brute
US Recruiting Poster, c.1917

General Pershing in France
Pershing: 'Damn! If only Wilson and Teddy were here we could at least play a game of cards!'
Kladderadatsch (Berlin), 1916

111

The Theatre of War
F.H.Townsend, *Punch*, 7 March 1917

In February 1917 the German forces on the Western Front had begun to withdraw to their newly built Hindenburg Line of defenceworks, destroying everything they encountered in a 'scorched earth' tactic. They had completed this by April when British-led forces opened the Battle of Arras to lure German troops away from the Aisne River sector where a massive attack was about to be launched by the French General Robert Nivelle who had replaced General Joffre as Allied Chief-of-Staff in December 1916.

After a five-day bombardment considerable gains were made by the British, and Canadian troops also took the important area known as Vimy Ridge. Losses were high – there were 32,000 casualties in the first three days (including the poet Edward Thomas who was killed on the first day of the battle) and the Royal Flying Corps suffered badly at the hands of superior German aircraft and tactics. However, it was seen as a limited success until deadlock set in.

When the main Nivelle Offensive began on 16 April there was considerable unrest. This major attack – on the 40-mile sector between Soissons and Rheims – aimed to take the important ridge known as Chemin des Dames. However, the Germans had found out about their plans and were well dug in. As a result French losses were huge – some 187,000 casualties by the end of the offensive in May – and this led to a mutiny by the French Army. Eventually half the entire French Army refused to fight and there were 30,000 desertions. In consequence, Nivelle was sacked in May and replaced by General Pétain, the hero of Verdun, who quickly resolved the situation (though only 50 men were executed at a time when mutiny and desertion were capital offences).

In the up-beat drawing by Townsend *(above)*, *Kamerad* is German for 'Comrade' and was the expression used by German troops when they wished to surrender. 'New Generation' *(left)*, by contrast, reveals the depressed mood of the French nation prior to the army mutinies.

NOUVELLE GÉNÉRATION

New Generation
'And you, my little friend, what will you do when you are 20?'
'I will die for my country, sir!'
Le Canard Enchaîné, 29 November 1916

The Return of the Conqueror
Edmund J.Sullivan, *The Kaiser's Garland* (1915)

British poster, 1915

For France, Pour Out Your Gold – Gold Fights For Victory
French Poster, 1915

Philippines poster, c.1917

A method used by both sides in the conflict to raise money for the war effort was by issuing War Loans or Liberty Bonds. These were public debt bonds which could be bought by institutions or individual investors in varying denominations and were to be repaid by the Government with interest. A considerable amount of the cost of the war (which began at £3 million a day in the UK alone) was paid for out of money raised by war loans. When Chancellor Bonar Law introduced Britain's second war loan campaign in February 1917 it was noted that an anagram of his name was 'War Loan B'.

REMEMBER · BELGIUM ·

Buy Bonds
Fourth
Liberty
Loan

US poster, 1918

The Last Strike is the Eighth War Loan
German poster, c.1917

Do Your Whole Duty!
Italian poster, nd.

Subscribe to the Sixth War Loan
German poster, c. 1917.

A Miner Success
'They must 'ave 'ad some good news or somethin',
Alf; you can 'ear 'em cheerin' quite plain.'
Bruce Bairnsfather, *Bystander*, 1917

The English Effort
John Bull punishes Germany. 'To be or not to be?' (Shakespeare)
Lucien Métivet, *Le Rire* (Paris), 1917

After the failure of the French Nivelle Offensive on the Western Front which left the French Army in disarray, British Field Marshal Sir Douglas Haig launched an attack against the 150-high Messines Ridge near Ypres in southwest Belgium. This was in preparation for a major new offensive stretching between the North Sea and the Lys River and aimed at breaking through the German lines around Ypres and then heading north to capture the ports of Ostend and Zeebrugge (this would later be called the Third Battle of Ypres or Passchendaele). The attack began on 7 June 1917 when 19 huge mines (a million pounds of explosive) – dug 100 feet under the German lines over the previous two years – were exploded. 10,000 German troops were killed almost instantly in the blast and 7500 were taken prisoner, many of them completely stunned, dazed and shell-shocked. Indeed, such was the power of the gigantic explosion that Lloyd George heard it at No.10 Downing Street in London.

The Third Battle of Ypres was launched (with French and Canadian support) on 31 July after a huge bombardment of German positions around the city. However, it was repeatedly held up by incessant rain which turned the countryside – already heavily cratered by shelling – into an appalling mud-filled landscape that made progress extremely heavy-going (some troops even drowned in the mud). The Allies were also hampered by the new German weapon of mustard gas. Eventually the offensive ended on 6 November when its final objective – the German-held village of Passchendaele outside Ypres – fell to the Allies.

Portugal
A. Schmidhammer, *Jugend*, 18 March 1916

Also fighting on the Western Front in mid-1917 was the Portuguese Expeditionary Force under General de Alorn. Germany had declared war on Portugal on 9 March 1916 and eventually some 100,000 Portuguese troops saw service in Flanders (serving in the same sector as the BEF), and in Africa. This German cartoon *(left)* has John Bull shovelling his Portuguese lapdog into the furnace of war (note the skulls of former allies on the floor).

Meanwhile, on the Eastern Front, domestic unrest in Russia caused major problems for the Allies. Food and fuel shortages, combined with dissatisfaction with the autocratic style of government of Tsar Nicholas II, led to riots in March and demands for more democracy. Within days 25,000 workers went on strike and when Imperial Army troops were ordered to fire on a demonstration they refused. In Petrograd (then the capital of Russia) the garrison rebelled, and the Tsar ordered the dissolution of the Duma (or Parliament). These events were the beginning of the 'February Revolution' (the Russian calendar was 11 days behind the Western one) which quickly spread throughout the country and soon afterwards the Tsar abdicated and a new provisional government was set up by Alexander Kerensky (Minister of War) with Prince Lvov as its nominal head.

In June General Brusilov was appointed Commander-in-Chief of the Russian Army but already troops, incited by the newly formed left-wing workers' councils (or soviets), were beginning to rebel. None the less, at Kerensky's request Brusilov began a major offensive towards Lemberg in Galicia (the Kerensky Offensive). After initial success, unrest amongst the Russian troops caused problems, and realising this the Germans launched a counteroffensive in August towards the port of Riga (capital of Latvia and the Russian Empire's second largest Baltic port). Using a new tactic – employing a brief bombardment followed by an assault with fast-moving lightly-armed 'stormtroopers' and mobile artillery – they had tremendous success, taking 9000 Russian prisoners (many more simply deserted).

The defeat at Riga – which opened the route to Petrograd, only 100 miles away – gave the Allies grave concern for the future ability of the Russian Army to wage war, especially as there was by now widespread disaffection within its officer corps, a fact satirised by the German cartoon shown here *(above right)*.

Entente Help for Russia
'Don't make such silly grimaces, Ivan! We are not hurting you.
We are only propping you up for fear of a breakdown.'
Kladderadatsch (Berlin), 1917

The Counterblast
Kaiser: **'Had a glorious time on the Eastern Front.'**
Hindenburg: **'A little louder, All-Loudest. I can't hear you for these cursed British guns in the West.'**
F.H.Townsend, *Punch*, 8 August 1917

A Nightmare
F.C.Gould, *Westminster Gazette*, 1916

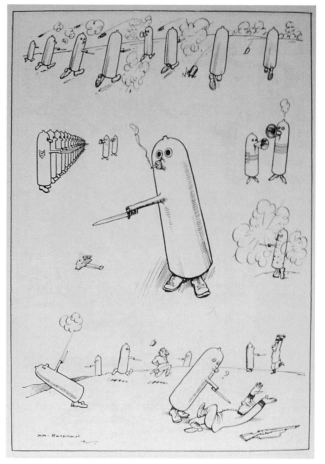

Will It Come to This?
H.M.Bateman, 1916

His Fatal Beauty
Old Bill: 'My wife married me for love, ye know, Bert.'
Bert (after prolonged and somewhat pained scrutiny of Bill's face):
'I had been wonderin' what it was, Bill!'
Bruce Bairnsfather, *Bystander*, 1917

Along with poison gas, barbed wire and flame-throwers, one of the most significant inventions of the Great War was the tank or self-propelled tracked gun (an idea that originated with Leonardo da Vinci in the 15th century and featured in pre-war science fiction by H.G. Wells and Jules Verne). Developed in Britain as a means to break out of the stalemate of trench warfare, the Germans were taken completely by surprise when they were first used on 15 September 1916 at Flers-Courcelette (two French villages they captured) as part of the First Battle of the Somme. However, only 32 took part and they had limited success. The British Tank Corps was formed in July 1917 and they were later used *en masse* by Sir Douglas Haig at the important railhead at Cambrai in Picardy on 20 November 1917, when 378 tanks and 8 infantry divisions attacked the German lines. This was a considerable success, with 10,000 Germans being captured for only 1500 British casualties and five miles of territory being gained over a five-mile front. After the Battle of Cambrai church bells were rung in London for the first and only time in the war.

Cambrai
'No stone will remain on top of another. That will be a splendid way to build a peace with Germany'
Wilhelm Schutz, *Simplicissimus* (Munich), 5 November 1918

US recruiting poster, 1918

The original British tank design was very slow-moving. Weighing 28 tons and with a top speed of 4mph and a crew of eight it came in two versions, 'male' and 'female' (depending on whether they were armed with 6lb canon or just machine-guns). There was later a lightweight variant, known as the Whippet tank. (The French – and to a very small extent, the Germans – also used tanks.) At first the construction of tanks – or 'landships' – was top secret (they were called 'tanks' to disguise their true nature when being transported to the Front – most believed they were to be used to hold water). As a result, the paucity of information allowed to the press by British Government censors meant that it was some time before their true appearance could be described for the public back in Britain.

This confusion is evident in the cartoon by F.C.Gould *(opposite, top left)*. However, by the time of Cambrai their appearance was well-known and their destructive force is commented on in the German cartoon *(above left)* where John Bull sets Cambrai ablaze. (The Black Tomcat featured in the US poster *[above right]* was the mascot of the US Tank Corps.)

The Reverse of the Medal
Optimistic German (reading paper): 'This is *kolossal*! Our irrepressible
airmen have again, for the twentieth time, destroyed London.'
Gloomy ditto: 'That being so, let's hope they'll stop those cursed
British airmen from bombing our lines every day and night.'
F.H.Townsend, *Punch*, 19 September 1917

Touch and Go
E.G.O.Beuttler, *The Merry Mariners* (1917)

While the tanks began to prove their worth on the ground other
technological developments were taking place in the air. By October
1917 – after a disastrous raid over Britain when 11 Zeppelins were
either destroyed (by air defences or storms), crashed or were
captured – the airship began to look a spent force and thereafter
the Germans largely relegated them to naval escort duties.
By contrast far more attention was now being paid to the
development of the aeroplane.

The Cards of War
At the Storks Squadron
'You will lose, Germania. Your kings are but knaves and I have
all the aces!'
Lucien Métivet, *Le Rire* (Paris), 1917

Originally only used by both sides for photographic reconnaissance
and as a target-spotter and range-finder for artillery, it soon developed
new roles. At first it was the Germans who led the field. Using a
Fokker monoplane fitted with an interrupter gear that allowed a
machine-gun to be fired through its propeller, the German pilot Max
Immelmann turned his aircraft into a fighter, shooting down his first
plane in August 1915 and dominating the skies for the coming months.
This so-called 'Fokker Scourge' over the Western Front was only
halted by the development of new, faster, Allied planes with similar
equipment.

1916 saw rapid advances in the new field of aerial warfare – this
year Lieutenant Leefe Robinson became the first airman ever to win
a Victoria Cross (for shooting down an airship), two Austro-Hungarian
flying-boats became the first aircraft to sink a submarine (the French
boat *Foucault*), at Kut-el Amara food supplies were air-dropped onto
the besieged Allied garrison, and the first long-range daylight attack
on London by German Gotha bombers took place on 28 November
(10 civilians were wounded).

This paved the way for much more concentrated efforts. In 1917
there were more long-range German bomber attacks on London
(notably a daylight raid in June when 14 Gothas killed 104 civilians
and wounded more than 400) and the Allies in turn bombed the
Central Powers.

Also in 1917, there were many complaints about inadequate
production of fast and well-armed aircraft by the Allies. This came to
a head in Bloody April when the British alone lost 150 aircraft and
316 aircrew, and the life expectancy of a new pilot was only 11 days
from the time he reached his squadron.

However, the arrival of new Allied aircraft and increasing successes by such skilled 'aces' as the Canadian Billy Bishop VC (72 victories) and the British Edward 'Mick' Mannock (73 victories) soon began to turn the tide. (The ace system had originally been introduced in France in 1915 to honour Adolphe Pégoud, the first pilot to shoot down five aircraft.) As a result, in July 1917 Germany reorganised its own fighter squadrons into larger wings of up to 50 aircraft. The most famous of these was the 'Flying Circus' led by the celebrated German fighter ace, Baron Manfred von Richthofen. Known as the 'Red Baron' from the colour of his aircraft (at first an Albatros and later a Fokker Triplane), Richthofen was credited with 80 victories before he was killed on 21 April 1918.

The French cartoon (opposite, bottom) alludes to the élite No.12 Group de Chasse fighter unit, better known as *Les Cigognes* ('The Storks'), one of whose stars was René Fonck, who joined the group in April 1917 and would become France's top fighter ace with 75 victories by the end of the war. Drawn by Lucien Métivet (1863-1932) it shows Marianne of France playing cards with Germania of Germany.

The cartoon (above right) by the Australian artist Will Dyson (1880-1938) was reproduced over the whole back page of the *Daily Mail* on 1 January 1915 under the heading 'Striking War Cartoon by Will Dyson' who the caption-writer described as 'a young man with the most virile style of any British cartoonist'.

Meanwhile, Beuttler (opposite, top right) has a seaplane upsetting the observation car of a Zeppelin and note that in the Townsend cartoon (opposite, top left) the German civilians are still celebrating the victory of the Riga offensive. Gould (right) has the Kaiser dressed as Shakespeare's Macbeth in a reference to his impending defeat in battle (like Birnam Wood, the Allied aircraft are made of wood).

The Aeroplane Shortage
The Kaiser (to Hun Airman): 'Don't go too near Whitehall, you might hit the people in charge of the British air forces – and we can't spare them!'
Wilton Williams, *London Opinion*, 21 July 1917

Wonders of Science!
Will Dyson, 1914

Seeing Stars
Macbeth: 'The cry is still "They come!"'
F.C.Gould, *Westminster Gazette*, 1918

The bombing of German cities was not the only headache that the German government had in 1917. In an effort to stave off Germany's growing revolutionary movement which had been encouraged by the situation in Russia, there were also heated arguments by Socialist elements in the Reichstag for electoral reforms and restrictions on the autocratic power of the Kaiser. Former Reichstag Deputy Karl Liebknecht of the revolutionary Spartacus League was imprisoned in 1917 and eventually the Chancellor, Bethmann-Hollweg, resigned and was replaced in July 1917 by Dr George Michaelis (who was himself replaced in November by Georg von Hertling).

Britain also had its own measure of civil unrest in 1917 when 250,000 engineers went on strike on 1 May. Similar stoppages also took place amongst Welsh miners (200,000 on strike in July 1915), Clyde shipbuilders (1916), munitions workers (1918) and others. In all, from 1915 to the end of the war it is estimated that 17 million working days were lost to industrial action in the UK.

The Kaiser's Friend
'Who goes there?'
'Clyde Striker!'
'Pass, Friend!'
Bert Thomas, *London Opinion*, 8 April 1916

Mac, *Cape Times*, 1917

Though the German-led Riga Offensive had gone well on the Eastern Front, the Central Powers were still embattled on the Western Front, with the Hindenburg Line being breached by the tank attack at Cambrai and resulting in 11,000 troops being captured by the British. The French also continued to hold out at Verdun at the cost of huge numbers of German lives (Verdun was never taken during the war). However, the Central Powers were having considerably more success against the Italians in the south.

Ever since entering the war, Italy had been trying to reach the important Turkish port of Trieste, only 15 miles from the Isonzo river. In no less than 11 offensives on the Isonzo the total number of casualties on both sides had been more than a million men. In October 1917, German and Austrian troops counterattacked and completely routed the Italians at Caporetto. It was a catastrophic defeat – the Italians lost 10,000 killed and 30,000 wounded, while 293,000 were taken prisoner and more than 400,000 troops simply deserted. Such was the impact of Caporetto on Italian morale that Italy's Prime Minister, Paolo Boselli, resigned and was replaced by Vittorio Orlando.

In Wilton Williams' cartoon *(right)* a rather threadbare Germania is unconvinced by the blandishments of 'William the Druggist' (the Kaiser's family name was Hohenzollern). By contrast the Italian war loans poster *(below)* has a female figure representing Italy holding Germany at bay, personified as an ancient Goth.

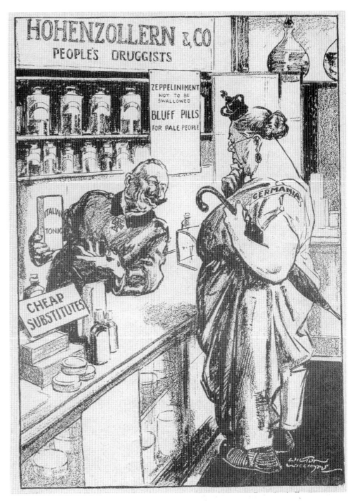

The Old 'Just as Good' Fraud
Frau Germania: 'But the only things that will do me any good are Western Front victories.'
William the Druggist: 'Ah! those we cannot get. But these Italian Tonics are just as good, I assure you!'
Wilton Williams, *London Opinion*, 17 November 1917

Subscribe to the Loan
Giovanni Capranesi, Italian War Loan Poster, c.1917

From Our Toybox
Lustige Blätter, 1915

A Few Suggestions for New Popular Toys
Thomas Maybank, *Passing Show*, 4 March 1916

Suggested Punishments for the Kaiser – No.2
To be made to inwardly digest the *Daily Graphic* war cartoons
Jack Walker, *The Daily Graphic Special War Cartoons, No.7* (1915)

These two cartoons *(above)* by German and British artists are so similar that one must have been drawn in response to the other. And, as they are a year apart it is to be assumed that the German drawing was the original. The figures in the German drawing are (left to right, top to bottom): an Italian Wobbly Man, Joffre with his Offensive Wheelbarrow (going nowhere), a Russian Steamroller (only goes backwards), Kitchener in a New Wargame (as soon as the centre of the pyramid is hit England falls to its knees), George V falling off a Bucking Horse, Wilson as the American Notes and Munitions Man, and Stuffed Puppets of British, French and Russian politicians from Pre-war Christmases (including Churchill next to the British Lion).

'Thomas Maybank' was the pseudonym of Hector Thomas Maybank Webb (1869-1929) who was perhaps best known for creating the children's comic character 'Uncle Ooojah', a huge elephant in striped pyjamas which appeared in a strip in the *Daily Sketch* and continued to be drawn by another artist after his death and survived until the 1950s.

A novel idea for torturing the Kaiser is suggested by Jack Walker *(left)* whose collections of cartoons had sold extremely well (600,000 copies of the first five volumes by the end of 1915). 'H.I.M.' stands for 'His Imperial Majesty' and also puns on the German poem 'The Hymn of Hate'. The Kaiser was in fact very affected by British cartoons and threatened retribution against *Punch* artists (amongst others) should Germany win the war.

Although in August 1914 there had been widespread enthusiasm for the war, not everyone was of this opinion. The celebrated playwright George Bernard Shaw had been vehemently opposed to the war, published many newspaper and magazine articles against it and gave many speeches decrying it. On 24 November 1914 his essay *Commonsense About the War* was published as a special supplement to the *New Statesman* and caused a huge controversy. Newspapers told their readers to boycott his plays and libraries and bookshops removed his works from their shelves.

Pacifists, conscientious objectors and others who opposed the war on ideological, moral or religious grounds (such as the Quakers) also had a hard time of it and were often treated harshly by their compatriots. Many served in non-combatant military positions such as medical orderlies, cooks or labourers but others who refused to take any part at all were often imprisoned. Amongst these was the eminent philosopher Bertrand Russell, who lost his job as a lecturer and was sentenced to six months' imprisonment for writing a pacifist article.

In H.M.Bateman's cartoon *(right)* note the white feather (for cowardice) in Shaw's cap, the Victoria Cross lying in the dust, the complete lack of military discipline amongst the troops and their slovenly appearance (Shaw even has unmatching boots).

If Bernard Shaw Had Commanded the Army
H.M.Bateman, 1917

Stage Manager: 'The elephant's putting up a very spirited perfomance tonight.'
Carpenter: 'Yessir. You see, the new hind-legs is a discharged soldier, and the front legs is an out-and-out pacifist.'
F.H.Townsend, *Punch*, 20 June 1917

**'You needn't be afraid, you imbecile,
Mohammed never eats pigs...'**
Louis Bouet, *La Baïonnette*, 28 September 1916

Last Reserves of the French 'Grand Armée'
Motto: For 'Civilisation' against 'Barbarity'
Lustige Blätter, 1914

Ready!
**Waiting to Pounce on All Hun Mischief-makers,
Whenever They Make Their Appearance**
Hindi Punch, 1918

Badges of Indian Army formations during the Great War

Colonial troops fought on both sides in the Great War, amongst the celebrated casualties being the father of the French Algerian writer, Albert Camus, who died at the First Battle of the Marne while serving with a French Zouave unit. It is ironic that the German cartoon from *Lustige Blätter (above right)* should make fun of French West African troops (the Tirailleurs Sénégalais) – note the card in the monkey's toes which reads '5th Gorilla Regiment, 1st Ersatz Battalion, Senegal' – as the Germans also had African troops fighting alongside them in German East Africa with considerable success.

The cartoon by Louis Bouet *(above left)* refers to the fact that many of the French colonial troops were Muslim (and hence did not eat pork), while the drawing from *Hindi Punch (left)* has a heavily armed Indian Tiger lying beside the British Lion. One of the intriguing aspects of some of the Indian formations was the use of the swastika, which many today only associate with the German Nazi Party. In fact this was originally the ancient Aryan sun symbol and predates the formation of the Nazi Party by many centuries. It was used on vehicles and noticeboards etc (never on uniforms) by soldiers in two Indian formations. The 6th Cavalry Brigade had a white swastika on a green background while the Euphrates Defence groups had a black swastika on a light-blue background. The other symbols are of a woodcock (adopted by the 14th Indian Division after 1917 when they were serving near Baghdad where the woodcock is common) and a panther (1st Indian Corps serving in Mesopotamia).

A Day's Work for L'Armée d'Afrique' and the French Colonial Troops
French poster, n.d.

Not Exactly What They Had in Mind!
Sultan Mehmet: 'Yes, I see, Brother, we have raised a
"Holy War" all right – b-b-b-but it's c-c-coming
the wrong w-w-way!'
E.T.Reed, *Bystander*, 28 June 1916

The Capture of Jerusalem
On the Hill of Golgotha
La Victoire (Paris), 13 July 1917

Bad Times for Robber Chiefs
Tiger Clemenceau and the British Lion Retire to the Jungle
Kladderadatsch (Berlin), 1917

The Turkish Defeat in Palestine
The Sick Man: 'Allah! Just see how I can run now!'
De Amsterdammer, 1917

The Allies continued to make advances in the Middle East and Anglo-Indian troops took Baghdad – Ottoman Turkey's southern capital – in March 1917. Then, when in June the British advance into Palestine was checked by the Turks, General Sir Edmund Allenby (known as 'The Bull') was transferred from the Western Front and took command. At the Third Battle of Gaza (31 October 1917) his troops carried the day and went on to take the port of Jaffa. On 11 December 1917 Allenby became the first Christian to conquer Jerusalem (the holy city of three religions – Judaism, Christianity and Islam) since the Crusades in 1099.

The Central Powers had hoped to raise a *jihad* or Holy War against the Allies by stirring up religious feelings amongst the Muslim population of countries in the Middle East, but in this they failed. The Allied cartoons show the true story while the German drawing *(above left)* shows the French and British, with their tails between their legs, in full retreat.

The Russian Hercules – and the German Hydra
Frank Holland, *John Bull*, 1917

The Pirate's Opportunity
The Struggle for the Wheel
Frank Holland, *John Bull*, 17 November 1917

The Breeze from the North
Will it Reach Berlin?
Le Rire (Paris), 1917

Order Reigns in Moscow
The Bolshevik: 'Only those? Pff! A band of fools and miserable creatures;
it is we who are the princes!'
Lucien Métivet, *Le Rire* (Paris), 1918

When the original 'February' Revolution (March in the Western calendar) took place in Russia most of the key figures in the future of Soviet history were far away and in some cases even out of the country. Stalin was in Siberia, Bukharin and Trotsky were in New York, and Lenin was in Zurich. On 10 April 1917, with the connivance of the German government, Lenin was smuggled across Germany and then via neutral Sweden to Petrograd in a deliberate attempt to destabilise the new Provisional Russian government and take Russia out of the war. (To counter claims that he had worked with the enemy – Russia and Germany were then still at war – Lenin invented the fiction that he had been transported in a 'sealed train'.) The plan worked perfectly and Lenin's train arrived at Petrograd's Finland Station in April 1917. In October a counter-revolution began when Trotsky (who had arrived in the city in May) led the newly formed Red Army against Kerenksy's government at its headquarters in the Winter Palace, Petrograd.

The government finally fell when Bolshevik sailors on the cruiser *Aurora* shelled the Winter Palace. Lenin then took power and moved the capital to Moscow.

The two cartoons by Frank Holland *(top)* comment on German involvement in the 'October' (November) Revolution. The three heads of the Hydra (one of the monsters that had to be defeated in the classical 'Twelve Labours of Hercules') of German influence are labelled 'Political', 'Court' and 'Military', while in 'The Pirate's Opportunity', the pirate is the Kaiser who climbs aboard the ship while a Bolshevik tries to wrest the steering-wheel from Kerensky. The prophetic French cartoon *(above left)* wonders if Russia's revolutionary fervour will spread to Germany itself, as indeed it would in the coming months (note the Russian royal regalia blowing in the wind as the Kaiser tries to hold on to his own crown).

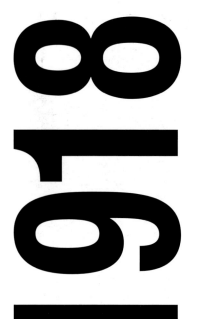

1918

AFTER FOUR LONG hard years of war the end seemed to be in sight for the Allies. However, at the beginning of 1918 the future was still uncertain – the French Army had mutinied, the Italians had been routed at Caporetto, Romania and Russia had left the Allies and only small numbers of US troops had so far arrived in Europe. Added to which, in the spring the German General Ludendorff launched the massive Michael Offensive in an effort to reach the Channel coast before American troops landed in force. It took the Allies completely by surprise and nearly changed everything. As well as breaking through at Arras and elsewhere, the Germans used huge long-range guns to bombard Paris from a distance of 50 miles. None the less, under Marshal Ferdinand Foch, the newly appointed Supreme Commander of all Allied forces on the Western Front, the Allies fought back and eventually halted the German advance at the Second Battle of the Somme. They later stopped four further German offensives in France costing Germany some irreplaceable 500,000 casualties in all, at a time when US troops began to arrive at the rate of 300,000 a month.

Meanwhile, the British were having some success. In 1918 they achieved air superiority in Europe after the formation of the Royal Air Force in April and the death of the German ace Baron von Richthofen and others. And in a surprise amphibious assault on Zeebrugge in Belgium – the main base for German submarines and destroyers operating in the English Channel – the harbourmouth was partially closed by sinking a number of old British warships packed with concrete. There were also successful major counterattacks on the Western Front with the French-led offensive at the Second Battle of the Marne in July, the British-led Amiens Offensive in August and the joint French/US-led Meuse-Argonne Offensive in September. Also in September the 'Allied Army of the Orient' had considerable success against Bulgaria and the same month British-led forces defeated the Turkish Army at the Battle of Megiddo in Palestine and later took Damascus, Beirut and Aleppo. The Italians also delivered a major blow to Austria-Hungary at the Battle of Vittorio Veneto in October (taking 300,000 prisoners) and 40,000 naval personnel of the German High Seas Fleet at Kiel mutinied the same month, leading to strikes and uprisings across Germany. At last it seemed there was cause for hope for the Allies.

Then suddenly it seemed that everyone in authority on the side of the Central Powers was leaving the scene – after the resignation of the Austrian, Hungarian and German Prime Ministers came the death of the aged Sultan of Turkey, Mehmet V. Then came the abdications of Ferdinand of Bulgaria, Emperor Karl of Austria-Hungary and even Kaiser Wilhelm himself who fled into exile in neutral Holland.

Leaderless and exhausted – and also now suffering from the first appearance of the 'Spanish Flu' epidemic which would kill 70 million worldwide over the next 12 months – the Central Powers soon fell like a pack of cards. First Bulgaria signed an armistice with the Allies in September, then came Turkey in October, and Austria-Hungary and Germany in November. Finally all hostilities ended on 11 November 1918.

A Peace Conference opened in January 1919, the German fleet was scuttled by its commanders while moored at the British naval base at Scapa Flow in the Orkneys and the end of the Great War was officially ratified by the Treaty of Versailles on 28 June 1919.

In a speech to the US Congress delivered on 8 January 1918, President Woodrow Wilson outlined his now celebrated Fourteen Points peace plan which would be the basis for the Versailles Treaty and would have a profound effect on international relations until World War II. As well as dealing with specific territorial problems the Fourteen Points included the renunciation of secret treaties, the establishment of 'freedom of the seas' (making blockades illegal), the removal of trade barriers, and a 'general association of nations'. This latter organisation (which would become the League of Nations) was intended to settle international disputes and Wilson argued that the principles of national self-determination as well as collective security should be paramount.

In this *Simplicissimus* cartoon *(opposite)* Wilson is shown as the Great Baal to which Marianne of France and George V of Britain pray for peace. (In the Old Testament the Israelites denounced the cult of Baal as heathenism and Beelzebub – or Baal-zebub – was the chief representative of the false gods.)

The Great Baal
'Lord, give us peace'
'First you must pay.'
Simplicissimus (Munich), 2 July 1918

How the Bolsheviks Made a 'Democratic' Peace
G.M.Payne, *Daily Sketch*, 1917

After the Bolshevik takeover of power in Russia it was not long before its new leaders made a separate peace with Germany, taking Russia out of the Great War in February 1918.

This was extremely good news for the Central Powers, as it released 44 divisions to serve on the Western Front, but was not as good as it had seemed at first for Russia. When on 3 March 1918 the two sides signed the Treaty of Brest-Litovsk, Russia had to give up a third of its population (including Finland, Poland, Belarus and the Baltic States – nearly all the territory gained by the tsars over the past 200 years), half its industry and almost all its coal mines.

Another Russian loss was the Ukraine, which had declared its independence in January 1918 and on 9 February had signed a peace treaty with the Central Powers. However, when German troops marched into the country – normally a very fertile land – they found that the retreating Russians had used a scorched-earth policy. The divisions of the spoils of the Treaty of Brest-Litovsk were also somewhat unequally shared between the Central Powers as is shown in the French cartoon *(opposite, bottom left)* featuring the Kaiser and Emperor Karl of Austria-Hungary. The first of the German cartoons *(opposite, top left)* shows Trotsky as a despot, returning to Petrograd holding a gun and a knout (the traditional symbol for oppression in Russia) to face any dissenting voices raised against the treaty. Meanwhile, the second one *(opposite, bottom right)* comments on the fact that by signing the treaty Russia has thereby cleared all its debts to the world.

Little Trotsky's Amusement
What Trotsky brought the Petersburgers from Brest-Litovsk
Kladderadatsch (Berlin), 1918

The German Mother Hubbard
Wilton Williams, *London Opinion*, 6 April 1918

The Russian Cake
'Here is your share, young Austro-Karl, and learn that in
German arithmetic two halves are never equal.'
Le Journal, 2 March 1918

Be Forgotten, O Ye Millions!
'Thus are our debts to the whole world cancelled.'
Simplicissimus (Munich), 1918

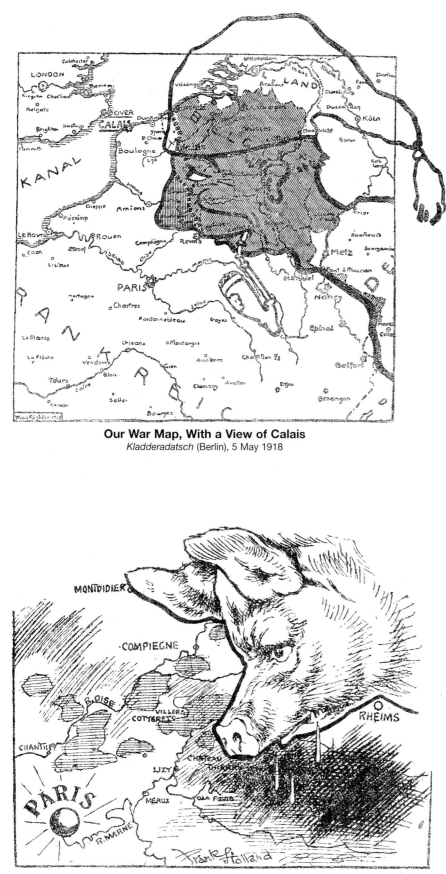

Our War Map, With a View of Calais
Kladderadatsch (Berlin), 5 May 1918

The Pig and the Pearl
As week by week the Huns progress,
You see the war maps in the Press;
But have you noticed that their line,
Suggests the vile snout of a swine?
Frank Holland, *Reynolds News*, 1918

The German Michael Offensive (named after Germany's national figure), was launched over a 50-mile front by General Ludendorff, Deputy Chief of the German General Staff, on 21 March 1918 with a huge 6000-gun bombardment. A million shells (including phosgene and mustard gas) were fired in five hours and after the guns came waves of storm-troopers. Also called the *Kaiserschlacht* (the Emperor's battle), the attack was boosted by the addition of large numbers of German troops from the former Russian Front and proved to be the biggest breakthrough by the Central Powers in three years (21,000 British troops were captured on the first day). The attack's main aim was to take the town of Amiens – a key railway junction between northern France and Paris – and then move on to the coast at Calais and hence England, with the intention of knocking Britain out of the war before US troops could arrive in force.

These two drawings from opposite sides of the conflict interpret the new frontline in their own ways – the German one has it as the silhouette of Michael with his eye on Calais while the British one sees it as the face of a pig with his eye on the pearl, Paris.

The advance of the Germans was rapid and was supported by large groups of aircraft including Manfred von Richthofen's 'Flying Circus' (when he was killed on 21 April 1918 command of his *Jagdstaffel* was taken over by Hermann Goering, who would become chief of the Luftwaffe in World War II). On 23 March 1918 three 'Big Berthas', mounted on special railway carriages, shelled Paris from 75 miles away (183 giant shells landed on the city – each taking 3½ minutes to get there) and the following day was declared a national holiday in Germany.

The situation for the Allies was desperate. On 12 April Field Marshal Haig even went so far as to command his troops to fight to the death: 'Every position must be held to the last man: there must be no retirement. With our backs to the wall, and believing in the justice of our cause, each one of us must fight on to the end.' However, though the Germans advanced 40 miles the Michael Offensive was eventually stopped on the River Somme. With the Germans' supply lines stretched to their limit and their starving troops suddenly halting when they found plentiful food in France, the offensive lost its momentum and in April it was finally called off. More than 250,000 casualties had been suffered on both sides.

The German cartoon *(right)* featuring a French cockerel sitting on a battered British lion's head alludes to the fact that on 26 March, in the middle of the offensive, the Supreme War Council agreed to make French General Ferdinand Foch co-ordinator (and the following month Commander-in-Chief) of all the British, French and American forces on the Western Front. In Sullivan's gruesome drawing note *(below right)* that the Kaiser, dressed as a fool, is dancing on the heads of dead German soldiers.

The belligerent French Prime Minister George 'The Tiger' Clemenceau insisted on 'war to the end' and kept up morale by attacking defeatism and dissent. In the German cartoon *(below)* from the Berlin magazine *Kladderadatsch*, the strident Clemenceau is shown chained to a figure representing Britain, who is seen as the real power. The drawing puns on the name of Clemenceau's paper which was briefly named *L'Homme Enchainé* before being renamed *L'Homme Libre*.

Under French Supreme Command
Simplicissimus (Munich), 23 April 1918

Clemenceau – A Man in Chains
J.Bahr, *Kladderadatsch* (Berlin), 6 January 1918

Dancing Partners
Edmund J.Sullivan, *The Kaiser's Garland* (1915)

The Austrian Ferment
Kaiser Bill: 'Shove like mad, Carl! Remember Nicky!
We mustn't let our skeleton get out of the cupboard, as Russia did.'
Wilton Williams, *London Opinion*, 2 February 1918

Drake's Way
Zeebrugge, St George's Day, 1918 Admiral Drake (to Admiral Keyes):
**'Bravo, sir. Tradition holds. My men singed a King's beard, and yours
have singed a Kaiser's moustache.'**
F.H.Townsend, *Punch*, 1 May 1918

While huge armies battled over the mainland of Europe there was still considerable activity at sea. On 1 February 1918, Czech nationalist sailors at Austria-Hungary's Mediterranean naval base at Cattaro (now Kota) on the Dalmatian coast staged a mutiny that had echoes of the one which had recently been so successful in Petrograd and had overthrown Tsar Nicholas II of Russia. And on 23 April 1918, St George's Day, the Royal Navy's Vice-Admiral Roger Keyes launched a surprise amphibious assault on the Belgian coast in an attempt to stop German submarines and destroyers from operating in the English Channel. In a daring raid, three ancient blockships filled with concrete were sailed into Zeebrugge and sunk across the harbourmouth to prevent enemy craft from leaving the port. The raid reminded some of the daring attack by the Elizabethan seaman Sir Francis Drake on Spanish ships and stores in Cadiz (1587) which delayed the sailing of the Spanish Armada against England until 1588. Drake referred to his action as 'singeing the King of Spain's beard'. Among those involved with the Zeebrugge Raid on Belgium more than three centuries later was the cartoonist Arthur Watts (1883-1935) who was twice awarded a DSO for his exploits.

The Marne
'I have been knocked about a bit, but I am still smiling!'
De Amsterdammer, 1918

In for a Pinch?
Newark News, 1918

Following the Michael Offensive the Germans tried again to break through the Allied lines but were finally halted at the Second Battle of the Marne in July 1918, suffering an estimated 168,000 casualties (the Allies lost 95,000 French, 13,000 British and 12,000 US troops). Seeing their chance, the Allied commanders then decided on a major autumn counterattack which was known as the Amiens Offensive, designed to recapture as much ground as possible. Led by Field Marshal Sir Douglas Haig's British Expeditionary Force and spearheaded by Australian and Canadian troops, the Anglo-French assault was launched on 8 August 1918 after a brief bombardment and with the use of 400 tanks and 1900 aircraft. However, such was the morale of the German troops by this stage that 15,000 quickly surrendered on the first day and many others simply fled the battlefield. General Erich von Ludendorff, who had once said that the British Army was comprised of 'lions led by donkeys', called 8 August the 'Black Day of the German Army' as it was their greatest defeat since the beginning of the war.

Over the succeeding weeks the German Army was forced right back to the Hindenburg Line by British, French and newly arrived US troops, and General Ludendorff (whose stepson had died in the Michael Offensive) became convinced that Germany could no longer win the war as it now had

The Conquering Hero
Frau Germania: **'Oh dear! Poor Wilhelm's won another victory!'**
(German newspapers are claiming their retreat as a strategic triumph.)
Wilton Williams, *London Opinion*, 1918

insufficient reserves of manpower and supplies for the task (he resigned on 26 October after showing signs of mental illness from overwork).

Wilton Williams *(above)* has a battered Kaiser trying to convince the German people that all is well while the Dutch and US cartoons *(top)* have the Crown Prince after being beaten by the French on the Marne.

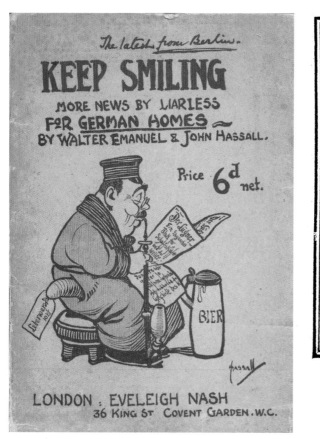

Walter Emanuel and John Hassall, *Keep Smiling: More News by Liarless for German Homes* (1914)

Jack Walker, *The Daily Graphic Special War Cartoons, No.4* (1914)

W.K.Haselden, *The Sad Experiences of Big and Little Willie* (1915)

S.Lupton and G.A.Stevens, *An English ABC for Little Willie and Others* (c.1915)

Here are some covers of British humorous books published during the Great War. The stepfather of John Hassall (1868-1948) was General Sir William Purvis Wright but Hassall himself failed to be accepted by the Royal Military Academy, Sandhurst. Renowned for his posters, in 1905 he set up the famous John Hassall School of Art whose many distinguished pupils included the cartoonists Bruce Bairnsfather, Bert Thomas and H.M.Bateman. Aged 46 when war broke out, Hassall served as a Special Constable guarding Buckingham Palace. ('Liarless' is a pun on wireless radio in Germany – note that the newspaper is called *Der Lüger* – The Liar.) The characters Big and Little Willie were created by W.K.Haselden (1872-1953) for the *Daily Mirror* and referred to the Kaiser and his son. They first appeared on 2 October 1914 and the Kaiser himself allegedly admitted that they had been 'damnably effective'.

Charles Grave, *The Hun's Handbook
for the Invasion of England* (1915)

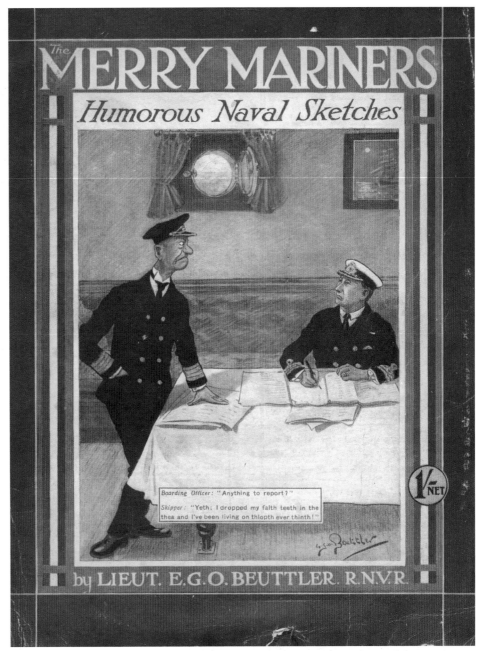

Lieutenant E.G.O.Beuttler, *The Merry Mariners* (1917)

Arthur Seymour and Ern Shaw, *'Good-Bye-Ee!'* (n.d.)

Edmund J.Sullivan, *The Kaiser's Garland* (1915)

'Have you noticed, Fritz, how our officers have stopped saying
"Onwards to Paris" all of a sudden?'
Raymond Pallier, *Le Journal*, (Paris) 18 June 1918

The Chastened Mood
Hindenburg *(To Germania)*: 'You've not quite caught the idea, madam.
What I rather want is an expression of calm and serene patience.'
F.H.Townsend, *Punch*, 7 August 1918

Peace
Berlin offers...Vienna proposes....Sofia demands
Le Rire (Paris), 1918

With there now being a distinct possibility that Germany might lose the war, the newly appointed Chancellor, Prince Max von Baden (a moderate deliberately chosen to give Germany an air of democracy), put out peace feelers to the Allies and asked President Wilson for an armistice based on his Fourteen Points plan. However, the Allies made it clear that no negotiations would be possible until the country's military leadership had been removed. Peace negotiations were also being contemplated by other members of the Central Powers group.

The cartoon by Townsend *(opposite, top right)* shows a crazed Germania (note the dachshund between her knees as she poses in a photographer's studio) starting to imagine the imaginable – that Germany might not win the war. It was inspired by a report that General Hindenburg had confided to a newspaper correspondent that the German people needed to develop the virtue of patience.

The Camouflage That Didn't
The Kaiser: 'You make a noise like a dove all right, but you don't look much like an Angel of Peace. Perhaps it's because the light's too strong.'
Prince Max: 'Yes, it must be the glare from the French towns we're burning.'
Wilton Williams, *London Opinion*, 19 October 1918

He Soon Found It
'Don't know the way? Wal, keep right on up this track till you come to a war. Then fight!'
Bruce Bairnsfather, *Bystander*, 1917

Alarmed at Last!
Kaiser: 'Mein Gott! The Dog has got a grip on me – and if the Eagle gets in his talons – I'm done.'
Melbourne Punch, 1917

On 12 September, the Allies launched an attack on the German-held salient at St Mihiel, south of Verdun on the Meuse River, using French colonial troops and soldiers of the First Army of the American Expeditionary Force (AEF) led by General John Pershing. The attack, which was the first major use of American troops in the war, was supported by 267 tanks and 1500 aircraft (commanded by US Colonel William Mitchell). It was a great success with 15,000 German troops taken prisoner. It was followed later the same month by a major new Allied attack on the Western Front, known as the Meuse-Argonne Offensive, by which the Allied commander-in-chief Marshal Foch intended to drive the Germans back from the Hindenburg Line. More than 600,000 men, including French and AEF troops, achieved their objective and the Germans abandoned the Hindenburg Line and by 4 November were in full retreat. The Allies continued their offensive right up to the signing of the armistice on 11 November 1918 but the cost was high, with 117,000 US casualties alone since the campaign began on 26 September.

In the gruesome German cartoon from *Simplicissimus (opposite)* US President Wilson tries to drag the figure of Death back into the bloody waters to fight on for another year.

Wilson the War-Extender
'Don't get tired now! Let's go on into a fifth year!'
Simplicissimus, (Munich), 30 July 1918

The Dummies
King Fox: 'What's become of his All Highness the Boss? He doesn't seem to have any use for us now!'
Sultan: 'I expect he's rampaging about in the Italian Alps – confound him! He's left me in a very awkward position!'
F.C. Gould, *Westminster Gazette*, 1918

As the Germans began to retreat on the Western Front, the 'Allied Army of the Orient' under the command of the French General Franchet d'Esperey launched a major attack from Salonika against Bulgaria in the south on 15 September 1918. Known as the Battle of the Vardar River, Skopje fell on the 29th and with its forces soon in disarray, Bulgaria surrendered and signed an armistice with the Allies on 29 September, the first of the Central Powers to do so. On 4 October Ferdinand of Bulgaria abdicated.

Meanwhile, in Palestine, British General Sir Edmund Allenby won a great victory over the Turks at the Battle of Megiddo (19-21 September), north of Jaffa on the Mediterranean coast, after the Desert Mounted Corps covered 70 miles in three days, taking 25,000 prisoners and leaving the route to Damascus open. The Ottoman Empire was now in disarray and on 14 October the deteriorating situation in the Balkans and elsewhere led to changes in the government of Turkey with the resignation of the Committee of Union and Progress (the nationalistic Young Turks group which had controlled the country since 1908). They were replaced by a new government led by Ahmed Izzett Pasha who immediately sought an armistice. Following negotiations on the Greek island of Mudros, Turkey agreed to end hostilities and to allow Constantinople to be controlled by the Allies. The following day General Cobbe, who had been fighting the Turks north of Baghdad, marched in to capture the important Mosul oilfields.

Gould's cartoon *(top)* shows the two 'dummies' ('Foxy' Ferdinand of Bulgaria and the Sultan of Turkey) abandoned by the Kaiser while Wilton Williams *(left)* has the Kaiser as the keeper of the Germanic Lunatic Asylum who throws his hands up in horror as Bulgaria runs away, with Turkey (and Austria) also about to escape.

Trouble in the Asylum
Wilton Williams, *London Opinion*, 12 October 1918

One Support Knocked Away
Rand Daily Mail (Johannesburg), 2 October 1918

A similar message is given in the South African cartoon *(above)* as a figure labelled 'Entente' knocks away Bulgarian support for the Kaiser. Meanwhile, Townsend's League of Abdications (a pun on the proposed postwar League of Nations), shows the deposed Ferdinand of Bulgaria arriving at the 'Hotel of the Kings in Exile' (in French-speaking Switzerland) where he is greeted by King Constantine I of Greece (who had abdicated in June 1917) who wonders how long it will be before the Kaiser himself is sacked.

HÔTEL DES ROIS EN EXIL

The League of Abdications
Ex-King of Greece: 'Hullo, Ferdie! Seen anything of William?'
Ex-King of Bulgaria: 'He's somewhere behind. He'll join us a bit later.'
F.H. Townsend, *Punch*, October 1918

A Visit to the Alpini
'The chauffeur says a car fell over here last week.'
'Oh!'
Bruce Bairnsfather, *Bystander*, 1916

Meanwhile, on the Italian border with Austria, the Italian Commander-in-Chief, General Diaz, launched a major attack against the Austro-Hungarian Army on 23 October. The Battle of Vittorio Veneto (so-named after the town which was its objective) also involved British and French forces and employed nearly 8000 artillery pieces. It was a great success for the Allies and by the end of the campaign on 3 November they had taken 300,000 Austro-Hungarian prisoners. The same day an Allied naval force captured the important Austro-Hungarian port of Trieste.

Bairnsfather actually visited the Dolomite Alps, Headquarters of the Italian Alpine Regiments, where he had been invited to draw sketches for the Italian Army. He was driven there by the Duke of Milan. ('*Pericolo di Valanga*' means 'Danger of Avalanches'.) The sniper cartoon *(below left)* was described by the US artist Charles Dana Gibson (creator of the Gibson Girl, President of the Society of Illustrators of the USA and later owner/editor of *Life* magazine) as 'the most brilliant thing Bairnsfather ever did'.

As the Allies advanced on the Western Front things began to look desperate for the Central Powers. The prophetic colour cartoon by F.H.Townsend *(opposite)* – featuring Mr Punch and the Kaiser in the roles of St George and the Dragon – was actually drawn in December 1914 for the almanac for 1915.

19...?
The war was over some time ago, but this man hasn't heard about it yet, and nobody can get up to tell him. His sniping is, therefore, very annoying to that Austrian village in the valley.
Bruce Bairnsfather, *Bystander*, 1918

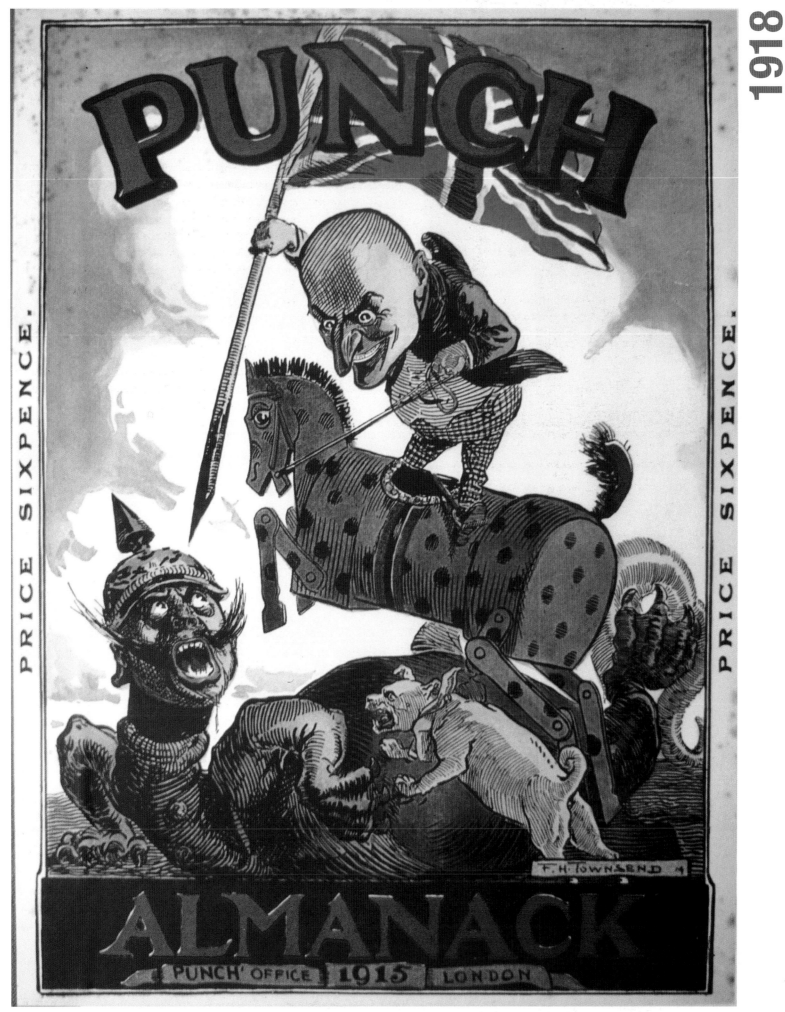

F.H.Townsend, *Punch Almanack for 1915*, December 1914

The Inadequate Mop
Wilton Williams, *London Opinion*, 28 September 1918

By the autumn of 1918 time had really begun to run out for the Central Powers. On 29 October 40,000 personnel of the German High Seas Fleet mutinied at their naval base at Kiel after the newly appointed commander, Admiral Franz von Hipper, decided that they should make one last foray against the British Home Fleet. The mutiny led to the taking of the city of Kiel itself and sparked uprisings across Germany which threatened to turn into a national revolution.

On 4 November Austria-Hungary signed an armistice with the Allies. Faced with chaos on the home front – as well as military isolation – the writing was on the wall for the Kaiser and Germany, which could not afford to fight on alone.

Sullivan *(opposite)* alludes to the Old Testament story of Belshazzar's Feast in which the conqueror reads the ghostly writing on the wall (*'Mene Mene Tekel Upharsin'* – meaning his time is up). Under the caption for the cartoon Sullivan repeats the text from the Bible: 'God hath numbered thy kingdom and finished it. Thou art weighed in the balance and art found wanting. Thy Kingdom is divided and given to the Medes and Persians' (Daniel V, 26-28).

Tempus Fugit
Jack Walker, *The Daily Graphic Special War Cartoons, No.3* (1914)

The Writing on the Wall
Edmund J.Sullivan, *The Kaiser's Garland* (1915)

The Bill
Louis Raemaekers, 1918

On 7 November a German peace delegation met Marshal Foch and Allied military representatives in a restaurant car on a railway siding in the forest of Compiègne, northeast of Paris and close to the Franco-German front line. (This same carriage was later used by the Germans for the signing of the French surrender in World War II.) Amongst the Allied demands were that German forces should immediately evacuate all occupied territory – as well as Alsace-Lorraine (which Germany had held since the Franco-Prussian War), that it should surrender all its submarines, warships, artillery pieces and machine-guns, and that Allied forces should occupy the Rhineland.

In Raemaekers' cartoon *(left)* death is portrayed as a waiter in a restaurant who hands the Kaiser and Prince Wilhelm the enormous bill for the war. Other metaphors are used in Walker's cartoon (drawn in 1915) and Townsend's cover *(opposite)* for the *Punch Almanack* for 1919 (published December 1918). In the latter (a remarkably prophetic picture of the Nazis' burning of books by Jewish authors and other so-called 'decadent' literature in the 1930s), the Kaiser and his son can be seen sheepishly burning a copy of a book labelled 'Machiavelli'. (Niccolo Machiavelli – from whose surname the adjective 'machiavellian' is derived – was the 16th-century Italian author of *The Prince* [1532], a standard text on power politics whose main theme is that any means can be taken to maintain authority.)

The Damp Squib
Jack Walker, *The Daily Graphic Special War Cartoons, No.5* (1915)

F.H.Townsend, *Punch Almanack for 1919*, December 1918

Victory!
Wilton Williams, *London Opinion*, 16 November 1918

'Deutschland Uber Alles'
Esquella de la Torratxa (Barcelona), 1918

'Unwept, Unhonoured, and Unsung!'
Frank Holland, *John Bull*, 1918

At 5am on 11 November 1918 – after 1586 days of war – Germany signed an armistice with the Allies. The fighting stopped at 11am that day. At this time German troops still occupied most of Belgium, all of Luxembourg and some of France and no Allied troops had crossed into Germany. (When the armistice was signed Corporal Adolf Hitler was recovering from a British gas attack and was in a German military hospital near Stettin.) The same day Josef Pilsudski became leader of an independent Poland and Emperor Karl of Austria-Hungary renounced his position as head of state. This prompted the creation of two separate republics – Austria and Hungary – on 12 November and a new independent republic of Czecho-Slovakia on 14 November (with Tomas Masaryk as its first president).

The loss of life and physical destruction of territory during the Great War had no parallel in history. It has been estimated that of 65 million troops mobilised by all the combatant nations, some 8½ million were killed and a further 21¼ million wounded with 7¾ million listed as missing or prisoners of war – 37½ million casualties in all. The figures for the Central Powers were Germany 1.8 million dead, Austria-Hungary 1.2 million, Turkey 325,000 and Bulgaria 87,000. On the Allied side: France 1.38 million, British Empire 908,000, Russia 1.7 million, Italy 650,000, USA 116,000, Belgium 14,000, Serbia 45,000, Montenegro 3000, Romania 335,000, Greece 5000, Portugal 7000 and Japan 300.

Also some 6.6 million civilians died, two-thirds of them in Russia and Turkey (of which 2.1 million were Armenian Turks killed by the Turks themselves in a campaign of ethnic cleansing against this Christian minority).

In Wilton Williams's cartoon *(opposite, top left)* the goddess of Victory has slain the ogre of Kaiserism and holds up the traditional symbol of success, a laurel wreath. The French cartoon *(above right)* takes a more cynical view, as fighting soon broke out again in parts of Europe in new and separate conflicts.

The Cessation of Hostilities
'As from the date of this decree, all fighting with cannon, sword or rifle that may take place in Europe will not count!'
Lucien Métivet, *Le Rire* (Paris), 1918

Tommy (homeward bound and determined not to disappoint): 'Why, Missy, three days before the Armistice the air was that thick with aeroplanes the birds had to get down and walk.'
F.H. Townsend, *Punch*, January 1919

The Tiger
Maurice Nardeau, *La Baïonnette*, 12 March 1919

President Woodrow Wilson sailed the Atlantic to participate in the Versailles Peace Conference which would be based on his Fourteen Points plan. When he arrived in France on 13 December 1918 he became the first serving US president ever to travel outside the USA.

The Peace Conference opened on 18 January 1919 at the Palace of Versailles near Paris but though delegates from many countries discussed the terms of the treaty, the losers in the war – Germany, Austria-Hungary, Turkey and Bulgaria – were not invited. In fact the discussion at Versailles only centred on Germany – there were separate treaties for the other members of the Central Powers later at Neuilly (1919, Bulgaria), St Germain (1919 Austria), Trianon (1920, Hungary) and Sèvres (1920, Turkey).

The delegates took three months to discuss the treaty's 440 clauses, during which time there was considerable animosity. French Prime Minister Clemenceau ('The Tiger') took issue with many of Wilson's Fourteen Points (at one stage he said: 'Even the Good Lord only had 10') and Prime Minister Vittorio Orlando of Italy and the Japanese delegation both walked out on different occasions. (Orlando was later forced to resign as Prime Minister because of his failure to win territory promised to Italy.) Even Lloyd George was critical of Wilson, recalling later: 'I really think that at first the idealistic President regarded himself as a missionary whose function it was to rescue the poor European heathen from their age-long worship of false and fiery gods. He was apt to address us in that vein, beginning with a few simple and elementary truths about right being more important than might, and justice being more eternal than force.' However, there was eventually a consensus and the draft treaty was given to the representatives of the German government for comment on 7 May.

The Germans complained that it departed from Wilson's Fourteen Points plan and were incensed to find that one clause specified that Germany had to admit guilt for the war (which had been started by Austria-Hungary's invasion of Serbia) and would thereby be responsible for huge payments (known as 'reparations') to the victorious allies. Germany could ill afford to pay such sums as its economy had been crippled by the war and the country was riven with social discord, strikes and uprisings. The treaty also deprived Germany of large parts of its 1914 territory and economic resources, as well as all its overseas possessions and seven million of its people.

Faced with such conditions, on 20 June 1919 the Cabinet of the new German Republic under its first Chancellor, Philipp Scheidemann, decided against signing the Versailles Treaty. One of the clauses of the proposed treaty had been that the German Navy should be handed over to Britain. Accordingly, the High Seas Fleet left Kiel and Admiral Sir David Beatty (who had succeeded Jellicoe as Commander-in-Chief of the Royal Navy in 1916) took the surrender at Rosyth in Scotland before it proceeded to the Royal Navy's base at Scapa Flow in the Orkney Islands. However, on 21 June, the day after the German government had refused to sign the Versailles Treaty, the German High Seas Fleet was scuttled by its commanders.

The Rough Model
'So far, good! I leave you with all these unfinished models. Now try to create something strong and lasting.'
Lucien Métivet, *Le Rire* (Paris), 1918

Preparing for the League of Nations
The Operators: 'See, Michael, the amputations are necessary in order to make it possible for you to dance with us at the Fete of the League of Nations.'
Kladderadatsch (Berlin), 1919

'And when shall we have the League of Nations?'
'League of Nations! We have it! It is we – against the Huns.'
Le Petit Bleu, 1918

For England, Home and Beatty
'Taking them over to Blighty! Tiddley-hiddley-hi-ti!'
Frank Holland, *Reynolds News*, 1919

The Skipper Who Skipped
Wilhelm the Skipper: '**I have piled my ship on the rocks, but I seem to have saved my own skin – for the present.**'
Wilton Williams, *London Opinion*, 30 November 1918

While the peace negotiations continued at Compiègne an uprising in Berlin led by Spartacists (German Communists) seized the Imperial Palace and proclaimed a Soviet republic while another group (the Social Democrats) proclaimed a socialist republic from the Reichstag. On 9 November, Kaiser Wilhelm II abdicated and Prince Max von Baden resigned as Chancellor. The following day the Weimar Republic was founded, with Friedrich Eisner as Chancellor.

Meanwhile, the Kaiser escaped to (neutral) Holland where he spent the next 22 years in some luxury in the castle of Doorn, living long enough to see the rise of the Nazis and the beginning of World War II (he died in 1941). Attempts by the Allies to extradite him and try him for war crimes were resisted by Queen Wilhelmina of the Netherlands.

In these two cartoons the artists imagine the Kaiser's life after the war. In the *London Opinion* drawing *(left)* the Kaiser, wearing a civilian hunting hat, relaxes in Holland (signified by the girl on the beach wearing traditional Dutch costume) as Germany's ship of state founders on the rocks. The Bateman cartoon *(right)* portrays him in a variety of unlikely jobs (this was drawn in 1917).

The Kaiser After the War
H.M.Bateman, 1917

The Peace of Versailles – The Child Enters
De Notenkraker, 1919

Peace and Future Canon Fodder
The Tiger: 'Curious! I seem to hear a child weeping'
Will Dyson, *Daily Herald*, 17 May 1919

Threatened with a return to hostilities, Germany eventually signed the Treaty of Versailles, exactly five years (to the day) since the assassination of the Austrian Archduke Franz Ferdinand that had sparked off the Great War. In a deliberate act of humiliation the ceremony took place in the Hall of Mirrors of Louis XIV's Palace of Versailles, where France had been forced to sign its surrender to Germany in the Franco-Prussian War.

This uneasy truce would prove to be the eventual undoing of the Allies. The Germans never felt that they had lost the war – their country had not been invaded, their troops had returned to Germany with their own transport and had been welcomed by civilians in a military parade in Berlin. In addition many of the new states that had been created by the peace treaties were inherently unstable with many internal ethnic divisions, and conflicts soon began to break out between some.

Added to which, many of Europe's new democratic governments were weak and unable to cope with the worsening international economic situation, giving opportunities for right-wing extremists such as Mussolini (whose Blackshirts gained power in Italy in 1922) and Hitler. And Russia had only escaped from the Great War to be plunged into its own bloody Civil War (1918-21). To cap it all, the newly formed League of Nations seemed to be powerless to prevent the outbreak of further international conflicts and within 10 years was effectively redundant.

Speaking of the Versailles Treaty, Marshal Foch, the supreme commander of the Allied Forces, said: 'This is not peace, it is an armistice for 20 years.' He was wrong by only 65 days. And there is considerable irony in the fact that the Treaty of Versailles, which had been orchestrated by President Wilson of the USA and was based on his own Fourteen Points plan, was never ratified by the US Congress and he himself was voted out of office soon after it had been signed.

Marshal Foch's perceptive views are well illustrated by the two cartoons shown here. In the Dutch cartoon *(left)*, Wilson (drawn as an old woman) introduces the peace monster. A huge, armed, adult man, dressed up as a cherub and holding a strangled dove and an olive branch, it is shown inviting the viewer into its embrace. Meanwhile, in Will Dyson's drawing, French President Clemenceau ('The Tiger') is seen coming out of the Versailles Conference with the Allied leaders President Wilson of the USA, Orlando of Italy and Lloyd George of Great Britain. The naked child weeping over the peace treaty at the left of the picture has above its head the words '1940 Class'.

Acknowledgements

As more than 70 years have lapsed since the first publication of the cartoons in this book (or the death of their artists) many are now out of copyright under international law. With regard to the rest, the Publisher and Author have made every effort to trace the copyright owners. However, as a great many of the publications involved have long since ceased to exist, and very little is known about many of the artists, it has not been possible to contact all the parties involved. Advice on omissions would be greatly appreciated and any further acknowledgements will be included in future editions. Meanwhile, the Author and Publisher would like to thank Park Art for supplying many of the images in this book and also the following companies and publications for the cartoons listed below:

Auckland Observer 40
Avanti! 24
Bystander 32, 48, 64, 68, 73, 84, 97, 100, 116, 118, 128, 142, 146
Cape Times 122
Chicago Daily News 24
Critica 31
Daily Chronicle 68
Daily Graphic 18, 23, 26, 28, 37, 40, 41, 42, 57, 60, 98, 124, 138, 148
Daily Herald 158
Daily Sketch 132
De Amsterdammer 128, 137
De Nieuwe Amsterdammer 83, 91, 95
De Notenkraker 33, 68, 158
Der Wahre Jacob 66
Die Muskete 105
Esquella de la Torratxa 96, 152
Fliegende Blätter 16, 87
Hindi Punch 76, 126
Toni and Valmai Holt 32, 55, 64, 68, 73, 84, 88, 89, 97, 100, 116, 118, 142, 146
Il 420 96
Il Travaso 67
Jiji 105
John Bull 86, 110, 129, 152
Jugend 90, 103, 107, 116
Kladderadatsch 23, 76, 80, 104, 106, 111, 117, 128, 133, 134, 135, 155

L'Anti-Boche 31
L'Assiette au Beurre 15
La Baïonnette 105, 126, 154
La Victoire 128
Le Canard Enchaîné 112
Le Journal 85, 133, 140
Le Petit Bleu 155
Le Rire/Rire Rouge 14, 36, 43, 61, 104, 116, 120, 129, 141, 153, 155
London Opinion 64, 75, 86, 121, 122, 123, 133, 136, 137, 141, 144, 148, 152, 156
Loukomorye 96
Lustige Blätter 66, 101, 107, 124, 126
Meggendorfer-Blätter 43
Melbourne Punch 80, 142
Mirror Group Newspapers 138
Mucha 34, 41
Newark News 137
New York Evening Sun 94
New York Herald 98, 110
Numero 30, 36
Passing Show 82, 97, 124
Philadelphia Press 110
Pollinger Ltd (Estate of William Heath Robinson) 17
Puck 33
Punch Ltd 11, 12, 13, 18, 20, 21, 25, 48, 49, 52, 53, 54, 58-9, 65, 70, 72, 74, 75, 76, 80, 81, 89, 92, 95, 96, 100, 108, 110, 112, 117, 120, 125, 136, 140, 145, 147, 151, 153
Rand Daily Mail 145
Reynolds News 95, 134, 155
Simplicissimus 43, 68, 74, 75, 84, 94, 102, 119, 131, 133, 135, 143
Vanity Fair 11
Weekly Dispatch 37
Western Mail 89
Westminster Gazette 19, 118, 121, 144
The World of H.M.Bateman 4, 80, 118, 125, 157